# DOLLARS, DIAMONDS AND DEATH

*a John Mariner mystery*

---

## EDDY ROGERS

ISBN: 978-1-09832-357-8 (print)
ISBN: 978-1-09832-358-5 (ebook)

My latest work returns as a straightforward mystery novel. As with all my writing, it's pure fiction and not meant to portray any particular person or business. Of course, many incidents reflect events that I have participated in or have heard about. In such cases, names and descriptions have been changed to protect the innocent as well the guilty.

John Mariner has aged a few years but still practices law in Blanco. Texas. He's a completely fictional character. So is his wife Carla.

As usual, my thanks go out to my editors, Hal Switzer, my sister Laurel, and wife Pat.

I am especially indebted to Hal and his wife Sandy for suggesting the title and proposing parts of the story line.

As always, I hope you enjoy this one too!

Ed

# 1

Greg Robertson sure made a splash coming to Blanco county. I'd learned long ago to discount rumors that swirled around our town, and there were plenty about him. According to the tales that arrived at my office from clients and friends, Robertson ran a hedge fund in Houston to great acclaim, returning twelve per cent annually to his clients over a number of years. That was after a rather stout annual fee of two per cent, which made him a wealthy man. Actually, to call him a hedge fund manager was a misnomer. I'd call him an active money manager, investing his clients' money for the best returns possible with minimum risk, or so his website said. "Hedge fund manager" is a sexier term than "money manager," especially since active money managers are unpopular in this day of index funds taking over the markets.

I had a personal interest in Greg. One of the local realtors called to tell me she had recommended me to Robertson when he needed a local attorney to prepare an earnest money contract for a ranch he was buying north of Brushy Top off US 281 between Blanco and Johnson city. The biggest one around, more than 2500 acres, with a large main house and a small house for ranch employees. I never actually met him when he bought the ranch; I always worked with his banker and Rose Mendoza, his executive secretary. The purchase was easy, as he hired an adjoining rancher who was a realtor to do the inspection work, and Greg paid cash. I checked him and his firm out, and if I'd had any significant funds, I'd have turned them over to Greg to manage.

I say Greg because after the purchase he invited me to a "visit" and lunch at his ranch. A great day to go there, with the sky clear and the weather unusually warm for mid-February. Not hard to describe him. Tall, six-three, trim and dressed in expensive casual clothes. Hollywood good-looking, like all the investment bankers who are dependent on clients and their perceptions of their banker. He was an extrovert, exuding charisma. While he won me over immediately, I could tell that his easy style masked his desire to get something from me. He pummeled me with questions about Blanco and its prominent residents and officials, and I did a full brain dump on the people I knew and worked with, careful not to share any client confidences. The lunch was nothing but first class. European brews and canapes, then roast beef sandwiches with home-made sweet potato chips. Best roast beef I'd ever tasted. After lunch we got into his Ford F-250 pickup and toured the ranch. His pride ran over during the tour when he talked about his airplane and the runway he'd just installed. More on that later. The previous owner had done a wonderful job of maintaining the ranch. Cedar free. I departed after three hours a bit overwhelmed by the magnitude of his wealth, his ranch and his personality. I knew he used a bunch of lawyers in Houston, but he might need a local lawyer down the road.

DOLLARS, DIAMONDS AND DEATH

Greg's wife, Sara, was an enigma. A beautiful woman, ten years younger than Greg's mid-forties. Lithe, tall and athletic. A second marriage, but she was no trophy wife. Sara had attended Baylor, majored in government and then went on to Baylor grad school for an MBA degree with honors. I didn't meet Sara for a year after I linked up with Greg, and then I had only a short time with her. Greg had asked me to introduce him to locals, so I invited the two of them to sit at my table for the Old Blanco Court House annual gala. The gala's one of the few times that most everyone connected with the town and the county join together. I'm not intuitive when it comes to assessing people I'm introduced to. Sara, though, impressed me as intelligent and engaging. At the same time, she enjoyed being feminine and attractive, flirting at times on a selective basis depending on the male's status. I saw that again in full bloom when Carla and I were invited to a New Year's Eve party at their ranch. Blanco rarely had such interesting personalities to deal with.

Since Greg enjoyed hunting on his ranch, which he named the "GR2500", Sara rarely came to Blanco, instead enjoying the bustle of the Houston social scene. Occasionally I googled her name and found a pile of stories in the *Houston Chronicle* showing her partying at various galas, always dressed to the nines. I wondered whether Carla and I would dress differently if we had their money. Maybe not. Wouldn't fit in here in Blanco.

My relationship with Greg changed one wintry day in early March when he called and asked me whether I could represent him on a personal matter. Of course I said yes, and although he offered to come to town, I volunteered to run out to his ranch. I was to be surprised.

The trip only took twenty minutes, half of it driving on the ranch road itself up to the top of a big hill that overlooked the entire valley between Blanco and Johnson city. The home he built there was typically Greg. Out of place, it looked like a mansion that should have been in Park city, Utah, where the rich folks go to ski. Massive glass windows with exposed woods and decks on the outside. Given the heat and sun, most locals opt for porches rather than decks unless they can't afford anything else. The old homestead, Greg told me, had been redone completely and made into a guest house. Being eighty years old, the house sat in a low area surrounded by a large grove of oak trees where it was safe from the winds and where a well could be drilled without going too deeply.

I drove up to the big house. The front had a chip-sealed drive-way, and Greg had built a parking lot off to the side for people invited to big gatherings at his mansion. Expecting no one else, I parked in front since it was in the mid-40s. Greg bounded out and thanked me for coming. Acting always as the gracious host, Greg offered drinks and snacks, but having had a large breakfast at home, I declined. Greg took that to mean I was ready to get down to business right away. He had something on his mind and wanted to get to it.

"I want to make sure that what we discuss will remain between you and me. Okay?"

"Sure. You're my client, and professionally I'm bound to keep confidences."

"All right. Don't know where to begin, but suffice it to say that my marriage with Sara has been a bumpy road. Yeah, she's beautiful and we've had a great physical relationship, but she can be a real bitch. Should never have gotten married. Sara really wanted to be financially independent, so a year ago I gave her three million to make her feel more secure. That didn't make things any better. She's gotten into the diamond jewelry business, you know, selling not only fine jewelry to her friends and other rich people, but also cut diamonds as an investment. Her sales pitch is that diamonds are a perfect investment since they're small, hold their value, and they can be put in a safety deposit box. Gold and silver have maintenance costs since you have to have a custodian take care of bullion.

"Ben Reeder is an estate lawyer with the firm I use, Gray and Caldone. He's done the wills for Sara and me, and right now they mirror each other. If I told Sara that I'd changed mine, she'd be really pissed off, so I've decided to get this done here by you. I have two brothers, both successful and both younger than me. I want you to name them my beneficiaries of everything I have. If something happened to either of them, their families should get the money. Sara's gonna have to fend for herself but she's got plenty already. Besides, she's a beneficiary named on my life insurance policy along with my brothers. I'd like you to hold the codicil and keep it confidential unless something happens to me. My dad died of an aortic rupture when I was fifteen, so anything can happen to people. Will you take care of this for me?"

"Sure, but I need a copy of the existing will so I can make proper references in the codicil to the dispositive section."

"I figured you'd ask for that. Here's a copy for you. There's one other thing. I want you to be the executor. I don't want anyone, including my brothers, to know, so you're the only one I can think of to name. Would you do that?"

"Let me think about that. Normally I avoid writing up wills and codicils and then acting in another capacity, such as a witness or named executor. People might challenge that as a conflict of interest."

"I'll have to take that chance."

"Well, okay, but if you ever have someone else to take my place, please do so,"

"Agreed. Want to see what I do for a living?"

"Sure. What do you mean?"

"Follow me." We walked into the side of the house that holds the bedrooms, and in one, I was treated to an array of computer screens–four of them–and several computers.

Greg enjoyed presiding. "This terminal is a Bloomberg, the other two array the trades as they happen on the New York Stock Exchange and NASDAQ. The fourth one I use to do research, emails, and so on. I have five guys back in Houston hooked into these same terminals so we can compare notes and make trades as opportunities pop up."

"Impressive. I'm surprised to see a Bloomberg terminal in Blanco county."

Greg laughed. "The internet has given everyone so much more freedom. No longer matters where you are for most professions."

"True enough. I work at home occasionally. The downside is that we're always available twenty-four seven."

"That actually helps my business, especially when there's a meltdown in Asia." We sauntered back to the living room and front door. "Thanks for taking this on and keeping it confidential. When you have it drafted, I'll come to your office so we can get it notarized. I had hoped that you could do that in the next day or two so that I can get back to Houston."

That sounded like a dismissal, so I assured him that I could get the codicil done quickly. I thanked him and excused myself. On the way back to my office, I processed what I was doing for him and digested his life and lifestyle. Money doesn't make people happy. Maybe the opposite.

# 2.

Robertson's will was a typical big firm document. Forty-five pages, with all sorts of tax provisions and trusts. Since I'd seen similar ones, I found the dispositive section quickly. The will left everything to Sara, and if she'd predeceased him, first to any children they had, and if none, to his brothers. No children presently and from what Greg said, none were going to be produced.

I routinely warn couples that their leaving everything to a spouse holds certain risks. For instance, the survivor could leave his or her wealth to anyone he or she wanted, cutting out the ones the other spouse wanted their part to go to, especially descendant children. Particularly true if the surviving spouse remarried. As a result, I understood why Greg might have wanted to change that even ignoring the troubled relationship he had with Sara. As the main character in the movie "Four Seasons" said, "Marriage is a set of hills and valleys." Greg was in a valley that he might eventually crawl out of, but I had my marching orders.

True to my word, within a day I'd finished the two-page codicil, and he came in to sign it. He reviewed it quickly, and then we went over to Texas Regional Bank and got it signed and notarized.

"Gotta go. I'm due back in Houston in three hours," he said.

"Well, you'll have to speed to get there from here."

"Not really. You saw the asphalt landing strip when we toured the ranch. Just like the one LBJ put on his ranch. The aircraft you saw is a HondaJet Elite. I've got a pilot's license and got trained by HondaJet to fly back and forth. Both Sara and my insurance company insisted that I hire a full-time pilot certified to pilot the plane. I did that, but he's so expensive I've been hiring him out to my friends to fly their aircraft since mine is idle most of the time. I've got a mega-dollar life insurance policy, and the insurance company instructed me not to do a bunch of things like fly helicopters or ride motorcycles. The premium's higher with a fixed-wing license like I have, but not much. My pilot would have flown me up here, but I hired him out weeks ago to a guy who needed a substitute pilot for his HondaJet because his pilot was on vacation. Hope the insurance company doesn't find out.

"Lots of people are buying HondaJets. The one my pilot is working for right now keeps his in our hanger. One of Sara's best customers for diamond jewelry. A rapper named I4U2. Actually, his real name is David Steward. Not my kind of guy, but he's got plenty of money. I made sure the passengers don't do drugs or smoke weed in flight. The pilot's seat isn't separated from the rest of the cabin.

"I'll take off in fifteen minutes and be in Houston at my office two and a half hours from right now. Time's money in my business, and I can't be away from my terminals long during weekdays. I've got internet on the aircraft too, so I'm never out of touch. One reason I have a full office here is that I can stay here when the weather's bad. Never want to take chances flying."

"That's amazing. I'm jealous!"

""Next time you need to go to Houston let me know. We'll coordinate schedules and you can have a free ride. Seats five."

"You can count on me taking advantage of that." Greg strolled out of my courthouse office, and I returned to my mundane world.

The weeks passed, and I spent my time working on the usual— divorces, wills, probate, and court fights between friends and neighbors over trivial things. I always cautioned my clients not only about the monetary cost of litigation but also the emotional costs. Litigation puts the parties in mental turmoil, and lawsuits seemingly last forever. Dickens' *Pickwick Papers*, where the lawyers have forgotten what the dispute was about but still churn out filings for the court, still describes courthouses today. Notwithstanding my distaste of litigation, the project I was spending most of my time on was a pipeline suit. Preston King Johns, a local retired accountant and rancher, had the pipeline going right through his property. Unfortunately, the route chosen by Goliath Pipeline went right through the middle of his ranch. I, and everyone else, told him that Texas law gives almost absolute power to pipeline companies to condemn rights of way. Johns resisted the route selection, maintaining that the logical location was fifty feet south, where an old pipeline used to be. The easement for that had been cleared of vegetation since 1927, and there was a road beside it.

Goliath touted that it had changed routes 127 times for others, so Johns figured he could get the pipeline company to change the route, at least on his twenty-three hundred feet crossing. He spent literally months talking to the pipeline representatives. Goliath complicated matters by contracting everything for the pipeline's construction to third parties, including the companies charged with identifying the landowners and negotiating an easement with them. Took only a short time for PK, as he was known, and I to figure out that those guys had absolutely no authority to make decisions. Goliath could veto anything they promised. Maybe a good negotiating strategy for the pipeline but poisonous to us.

While Johns was negotiating for a route change, Goliath made a "final offer" which had to be accepted or a lawsuit would be initiated by Goliath. The monetary offer was a lowball offer, which the pipelines routinely do to set the stage for negotiating and coercing landowners into agreeing to whatever the pipeline company wants. Johns told me that his frustration level had reached a peak dealing with people who could only negotiate a proposal for submission to nameless people in Houston. So he ignored the final offer and a lawsuit followed. Not that Johns was out for more money. PK's concern was that in clearing the pipeline route, Goliath would destroy four or five hundred oak trees and a turkey habitat on the property, and of course PK wanted the pipeline to go where it wouldn't destroy so many trees, south to the old easement. The old pipeline, installed in 1927, had been removed five years ago.

The Goliath contractors PK had dealt with gave contradictory signals, saying at times they were diligently studying a move of the pipeline but other times saying that Goliath would never move the route. After Goliath filed the lawsuit, the next step would be a Commissioners' administrative hearing to determine the diminished value of the property caused by running a pipeline through it. Handling PK and his emotions justified my fee, the greater of my hourly rate or ten per cent of anything above the initial lowball offer. Litigation is an emotional rollercoaster. I didn't want to obsess over it; that was for my client to do. Still, gathering the facts, organizing

them and researching the alternatives, if any, took up a great deal
of time.

● ● ●

A full month after I took care of Greg's codicil, as I prepared
for Johns' valuation hearing, a panicked call came in from Sara
Robertson. I hadn't ever talked to her over the phone, but I took
the call figuring that whatever she was calling for was important.
Perhaps she somehow found out about the codicil.

"This is terrible!"

"What?"

"I think you know that Greg and I routinely go back and forth to
Houston in the HondaJet. Greg left yesterday afternoon for a quick
trip to the ranch to check up on our ranch manager's arranging
for a cattle sale. Gary Servring's his name. Our pilot's out again
on loan to a friend so Greg flew without a co-pilot. I'm in Houston
and Greg was coming back here, but fifteen minutes after takeoff,
the airplane took a nosedive into the ground. As far as I know
Greg was killed. The police told me that the plane crashed east of
Bastrop, in a heavily wooded area called the Lost Pines. The police
and EMS are there now, but the plane didn't burn. They said that
they'd notified the FAA and that someone would be out to start
an investigation. That was a safe aircraft. The weather's clear and
Greg never took chances flying. Can't figure out why it would crash.
What should I do—anything? Greg named me executor of his will,
and I have a power of attorney if he's hurt and in the hospital."

"I know that this is a difficult time. There's nothing you or I can do
right now. Let's wait and find out the facts, especially about Greg."

Everyone gets into a routine, not expecting a change of scenery. Then "Wham!", your life changes. I didn't want to tell Sara about Greg's codicil changing the will's terms, including naming me executor. I shouldn't have agreed to that, but I figured Greg was a lot younger than me and in good health. Besides, he said he didn't have anyone else he could trust with the codicil and its terms.

# 3.

The authorities found the wreckage of the airplane quickly, and as Sara had said, it didn't burn. Its crashing was the first loss of that type of aircraft. Falling into an area of pine trees, the plane itself was shredded by the trees, but the fuselage held its integrity. Greg was found dead, strapped in his seat. The crash and Greg's death made headlines both locally and in Houston, and a week later a huge funeral was held at St. Mark's Episcopal Church, a huge cathedral-like church in the middle of the wealthy section of Houston. Without making myself prominent, I went to the funeral and the reception following the service, but since I didn't know anyone other than Sara, after I paid my respects to her I quickly left. On the way out I introduced myself to Rose Mendoza, the woman I'd worked with buying the ranch. I figured I'd be dealing with her on Greg's estate. Pretty woman, in her mid-forties like Greg, but conservative looking. She had her hair pulled back in a bun and was in a blue linen coat with a white plain blouse. Hardly any jewelry. I'd not told anyone about the codicil, but I knew I had to address that and the probate right away. Rose would have to be an ally working through that.

I wished I could have filed the probate of Greg's estate in Blanco county, claiming that he resided here, but I knew that he had his home and firm in Houston, and the business information I would need, besides what was on his laptop, resided in Houston. And then there was Sara. How could I tell her about the codicil? The FAA and NTSB, of course, were working on discovering the cause of the crash. If the aircraft had a defect, a major cause of action against Honda would be an asset of the estate. I'd have to hire someone skilled in aircraft litigation, and those lawyers are in Houston. I consoled myself that my involvement in the out-of-town probate would produce prodigious fees since the original will provided for any executor other than Sara to be fairly compensated. Still, with the pipeline litigation and my other routine engagements, I'd have to work far longer hours than I really wanted to.

Sara called early Monday, two weeks to the day after the accident. "John, I wanted you to know before it hit the papers. The NTSB determined that the plane crashed for a simple reason. It ran out of fuel."

"How could that be with Greg being so careful about such an elemental thing?"

"Well, I don't know, but I do know that we don't have any refueling capability at the ranch. We always refueled in Houston or wherever the plane was going."

"We'll have to wait for the full report. Say, Sara, I need to meet with you regarding Greg's estate. Are you going to be at the ranch any time soon?"

"Not really, but then again, I need to get out of Houston. Everyone and their dog is calling, texting or emailing me about Greg or wanting me to work with them handling Greg's affairs."

"Nothing needs to be done right away. Should I come to Houston to talk to you? We could meet in Greg's office."

"That would be better if you have time. I know I should get away but I'm uneasy travelling right now."

"I understand. How is Thursday at one at Greg's office? That way we can meet, and after the meeting I can get back here to Blanco."

"Deal. See you then."

As you might expect, I didn't look forward to meeting with Sara and telling her about the codicil. I made copies but kept the original in my office. I didn't know Sara well. Pretty, with dark blond hair and perfectly white, too white, teeth. Greg said she was in a jewelry business that catered to rich Houstonians, but that was all I knew. I got into my pickup for the trip that Thursday morning, leaving the SUV for Carla. A wintry, somber, cloudy March day late in the month, with temperatures in the mid-50s. A good day to stay home with a fire in the fireplace. The three-hour trip wasn't relaxing, as I anticipated a stormy meeting with Sara.

Greg's office, of course, had to be downtown where the institutional finance business goes on, along with lawyers, bankers and accountants. I didn't miss going to Houston. Even before the lunch hour, the traffic was bumper-to-bumper. I parked in the Texas Tower's garage but then diverted to one of the underground restaurants, a sandwich shop, for lunch. No need for barbeque or Mexican food; I got plenty of that at home. Promptly at one I went up to the 71st floor. The firm had the entire floor. An expensive plaque next to the glass doors announced "Robertson

Investments", so I went in. An attractive young woman sat at the receptionist's desk and asked if she could help. She looked at me as if I didn't belong there since I had on khaki slacks, a blue blazer and an open patterned shirt. I hadn't been in a suit outside of courtrooms for at least a decade.

"I'm John Mariner, here to see Sara Robertson."

"Oh, yes, Ms. Robertson said you'd be arriving. I'll tell her, but meanwhile please step into the conference room to my left." I dutifully followed her into the room, which had an expansive view of downtown. Since it was cool outside, no one was walking the streets. Everyone walked the tunnel system beneath downtown. The view was spectacular even on a cloudy day.

"Hello, John. I hope you're well."

"The proper question is how you are doing, not me."

"I'm coping. I never thought that Greg might die, especially this way and this young."

"True. Totally unexpected."

"So I'm not sure what we need to talk through. I've already talked to Ben Reeder, and he has the original wills we did. He explained the process of probate to me and what I'd have to do as executrix. Thankfully I've got plenty of support here at the office to untangle everything, and I found Greg's passwords. He had everything on his laptop, which the NTSB recovered from the wreckage. They said they'd return it to me in a few days. I gave them the passwords. They wanted to see whether there was anything there that might explain why the plane went down. Sort of a technical autopsy."

"Sara, this is going to be hard for you, but things are different than you're aware of. Greg came to me two months ago and pledged me to keep matters confidential. He said you two were

having problems and that you were already financially independent, so he had me prepare a codicil to his will naming me executor—for lack of having someone else—and his brothers as sole
beneficiaries."

Sara sparked. I could see that she had a temper. I let what I said
sink in, and for almost five minutes there was silence in the room.
She sipped on a bottle of water, sat up in her chair, and tried to
act in a normal manner.

"That's quite a surprise. Could I see the codicil?"

"Of course. Here's a copy. I'll send a copy to Ben Reeder too.
Since I'll need local counsel in Houston to file the probate here, I'll
ask him to sign on as counsel for Greg's estate. Under the circumstances, he may see a conflict and decline to represent the estate.
There are plenty of good probate lawyers in town if that happens."

"I can't believe Greg would do this to me. Sure, we had our
troubles, mainly because we're both pretty headstrong and both
of us wanted to be in charge of the other." She gave a little chuckle.
"We did have a stormy set of arguments right before the date on
this codicil, and after that our relationship cooled a lot. We did
sleep in the same bedroom, but our physical relationship turned
non-existent. I was hoping that things would get better. Apparently
not. Greg was worried. He used to be warm and talkative. I felt that
he was taking out whatever was bothering him on me."

"Now you know why I wanted to meet with you. This isn't
anything that I could do over the phone. I'll leave you alone for a
few days, but to get Greg's estate handled efficiently, we'll need
to cooperate and enlist the people in this office to help us out. If
you'll give me the passwords, I'll contact the NTSB and get the
computer, telling them that I'm the executor. There's no hurry with

the probate unless you're in need of cash. I know right now that you're hurt and angry, so you need time to process where we are. I hope you'll sign on to helping me."

"The safety board people are still working on the accident. Here's the guy's name and number," she said as she wrote the information on a pad. "Give me a couple of days and then call me. In the meantime please set things up with Reeder. Thank you for coming all this way simply to give me the ugly message from Greg."

"If you don't mind, while I'm here I'd like to meet with Rose Mendoza. I worked with her when we bought the ranch, and she'll be involved in gathering information for the probate."

"Sure. I think I'll leave, but I'll have the receptionist get you Rose. She's nice and she's easy to work with."

"Thank you for understanding my rather awkward situation," I said as I stood up and she left room, not replying. Must have been quite a shock for her.

Several minutes later, Rose breezed into the conference room. "Hello again." Rose came in, dressed as conservatively as she had at the funeral, but this time the outfit was black, with the same white blouse. Well-kept and trim, she had a look of authority as she strode in.

"Good to see you again. The funeral was no place to be chatting."

"Sara told me that you two were meeting here. Is there anything I can help with?" I told her about the will and the codicil, omitting the codicil's background. "That's quite a surprise. I'm not sure why Sara wasn't named executrix."

"Greg made his wishes clear to me, so you're stuck with me."

Rose laughed. "We made a pretty good team when we bought the ranch. Actually I look forward to working with you again."

We said our good-byes, and I couldn't get out of there and out of Houston fast enough, knowing I'd have to eventually come back.

I called the official from the National Transportation Safety Board, the NTSB, on my way back to Blanco. Pat Carnegie. "This is John Mariner. I'm the family lawyer for the Robertsons and am the executor of Greg's will. I'm touching base with you to introduce myself and make sure I get the results of your investigation, along with his widow Sara. Also, I wanted to see when I could get Greg's laptop. I understand you recovered it from the aircraft. I have the passwords. I think most of the financial information on it is duplicated on the server in his office, but who knows."

"Thanks for calling, John. We're restricting our activity to the technical aspects of the crash. As you may know, we have the authority to call the FBI if an incident looks suspicious or we're undermanned. True on both counts in this case. They've taken the investigation over. The guy in charge is Oliver Stonewater. He's been to the crash scene and is working with us to figure all this out. He'll be calling you. We've looked at the laptop. Ms. Robertson gave us the passwords. So far there isn't anything on it that relates to the cause of the aircraft going down, so we turned it over to Stonewater for the FBI to do a deeper analysis. We haven't discovered anything to contradict the basic finding that the aircraft simply ran out of fuel. As you know, most new jet aircraft like the HondaJet have fuel gauges but pilots also rely on fuel consumption math to figure out how much fuel they have. We're going through the flight log to see when they last filled their tanks. Ms. Robertson said they usually refueled in Houston and not any other airport unless they were on a trip somewhere. I'll let you know."

"Thanks."

# 4.

The pipeline case bubbled up to the top of my schedule. Texas pipeline law dictates a strict routine for creating pipeline easements. First, the pipeline company sends a supposedly good faith letter to the landowner, saying they are going to run a pipeline through the owner's property. The letter makes a dollar offer. Unfortunately, the pipeline company has no motivation to make a fair offer, although legally they're required to do so. As a result, the initial offer is invariably a lowball offer that the owner, my client, declines. That's exactly what happened to PK. Then there's an administrative hearing in which three commissioners, by law required to be local landowners, hear both sides present their position on the decline in the value of the property due to the pipeline going through the property. In PK's case, the 2300 feet went right through groves of live oak trees and a turkey roost, so we claimed damage of over a million to the 250-acre ranch, bolstered by a report to that effect by a local real estate appraiser. Oddly, the law does not provide any compensation to the landowner for the disruption that occurs during the laying of the pipeline. Just the diminished value and nothing more, not even attorneys' fees if the owner gets more than originally offered.

The "hearing" wasn't the kind of judicial or administrative courtroom hearing that I was used to. We packed into a room at the local motel, a room that had previously been a standard motel room. The hearing lasted about two hours. They put their appraiser on, who submitted accurate financial information but opined that the diminished value was paltry, $75,000, because five years from now the land would have recovered. He didn't speak to the removal of PK's hundred year old oak trees, and that gave me the opportunity to showboat an impassioned defense of the four hundred trees when it came my turn. The commissioners dismissed us after both sides had spent themselves, and fifteen minutes later, we trudged back into the hearing room. The lead commissioner solemnly announced that the commissioners were embarrassed by the partisan presentation of Goliath, stated that they agreed with my presentation and awarded PK a million and a half. The Goliath group, visibly mad, stood up and walked out of the room. PK was ecstatic, but I warned him that the large award would only motivate Goliath to take us to the next step, a full-blown trial in Johnson city with a state court judge. Of course, to appeal the award, Goliath would have to put up a bond for twice that amount. Nonetheless, I told PK that such a large award would never hold up long term. Perhaps the large award would motivate Goliath's lawyers to come to the bargaining table. The award made the *Blanco county News*, and wherever I went locals congratulated me on getting the big award, not knowing that PK would never see that amount.

• • •

The week spent fighting Goliath burned up enough time for the NTSB to finish their initial investigation of the downed aircraft.

The laptop was on its way to me. I called Carnegie, and unlike most government officials, he answered the phone.

"I was getting ready to dial you. Our investigation is complete and surprising. The aircraft did indeed crash simply due to a lack of fuel. The odd part is that the flight log notes that the pilot, after his last trip, refueled the plane in Houston two weeks before Robertson's flight up to his ranch. As you know, the runway and metal building housing the aircraft are over the hill from the big house and the guest house. Fairly remote. The capacity of the fuel tanks is 375 gallons, and fuel consumption at cruising levels is 90 gallons per hour. The flight to the ranch consumed a little over a hundred gallons. The bottom line's clear. Someone drained the tanks after it was refueled in Houston. What we're having trouble figuring out is the fuel gauge. The fuel gauge was somehow modified to show plenty of fuel, though Robertson should have wondered why the fuel tanks showed nearly full the whole time. Like a car's gas gauge, the little needle should have been going down as fuel was consumed. When it crashed it showed almost three-quarters full. Pretty sophisticated. Robertson wanted to get back to Houston in a hurry so he took off anyway, thinking through the math that he had plenty of fuel.

"Someone murdered Robertson. Deliberate and not done by an unsophisticated hillbilly. That's why I passed all this on to the FBI, and they've launched a full investigation. Sorry to dump this on you. Someone has to tell Robertson's widow. Are you up to that?"

"Lots to process. I'm not sure why anyone would want to do away with Greg. He had an ideal life. I'll let Sara Robertson know right away. The FBI will want to interview her to find out who might have had a motive to pull this off."

"Thanks. When the written report is available I'll let you know."

"Thank you!"

• • •

I sat in my office digesting the conversation with Carnegie. Who would have wanted Greg dead? I supposed that Sara would be on the list, but I couldn't think of anyone else. Time would tell.

As I was rolling over everything I'd learned in my mind, the phone rang.

"Hello, this is Oliver Stonewater. I'm an FBI agent in the Austin office. I've talked to Pat Carnegie at the NTSB, and he briefed me on where we are with the plane crash. An accident morphed into a homicide. I understand that you're the executor of Robertson's estate, and Pat told me that he's had you handling Robertson's widow, Sara. Here's where we are. No suspects, but possible motives popping up. I checked with the SEC in Washington to review Robertson's investment advisory filings, and the agency has an ongoing investigation of Robertson and his firm regarding their handling of client money. They're going to do a full review of his books. His published returns, they say, look suspicious because of the consistency of his investment returns in spite of the ups and downs of the markets. Several complaints have been filed that he was not returning funds, but as soon as a complaint was filed, the complainant got his money back. Not sure that's enough to make someone mad enough to murder, but I'll keep you up on what's going on. Pat said you had information that would be helpful."

"Yeah. Awkward for me. The last time I was with Greg, he said he had marital problems going on and wanted to change his will.

Instead of leaving everything to Sara, he had me compose a codicil naming his brothers as beneficiaries, leaving Sara out entirely. Of course, she's still entitled to her half of community property, but Greg told me he started his investment firm before he got married, so that asset is his separate property. Since he wanted to keep the codicil confidential, he talked me into being the executor. I agreed to it simply because I thought the possibility of his dying was pretty remote. How wrong I was."

"That, of course, makes Sara a prime suspect. Any detail on their marital issues?"

"No, Greg didn't say what was wrong. I do know that Sara has her own business. She designs and sells high-end jewelry to rich people in Houston and Dallas. I hear the business is successful. Quite private. She doesn't advertise but gets referrals by word of mouth. That's one reason she didn't spend much time at their ranch."

"I'll look into that. The more we get to know Sara and what she's like, the more we can assess her as a suspect. Know what his business looks like inside? Like who works for him, who owns the business besides him, who his investors are?"

"Not really except that I've met and worked with Greg's executive assistant, Rose Mendoza. Greg said he originally made his mark in the investment community investing in Grande Oil Company, a natural gas exploration company that pioneered drilling by fracking. He and his investors made a bundle on that and then rode the wave as other companies learned how to do it. As coal became unpopular, instead of natural gas being almost exclusively a heating fuel for homes and businesses, natural gas consumption grew rapidly as gas turbines replaced coal plants to generate electricity. Sara said that's where Greg got the money for the big ranch here.

"As his business matured, Greg broadened his investment horizon to become an active money manager. His firm, Robertson Investments, developed a template for investing that, he said, smoothed out the ups and downs of the market by aggressive trading in things I don't have any familiarity with. Puts, calls, shorts, that kind of thing, in addition to equities. He also said he was into derivatives, whatever those are. I think he saw my eyes glazing over as he pontificated, so he quickly ended his story of what Robertson Investments did."

"Whew, that's more information than I was expecting. I'll send you my email and contact information. Next step is for us and the SEC to see what's going on at Robertson Investments. You can tell Ms. Robertson that we're focused on his firm right now and will share anything we find with you and with her."

"Thanks. By the way, is there a chance you might let me have the laptop for a week or two? I'm sure that it has all the financial information on the firm and on Greg's personal affairs on it. Need that for the probate proceeding."

"Okay, but I want it back. And if you find anything relevant to the accident, you need to let us know. Do you have a way to get the computer from our office here in Houston?"

"I'll get Rose Mendoza, Greg's executive assistant at the firm, to pick it up from you. I'll tell her you'll want a receipt. I'll get it back to you as quickly as I can."

I wasn't sure where this was going, but I knew I had to address the probate of Greg's estate soon.

I called Rose, and she retrieved the laptop from Stonewater the next day. I received it thanks to FedEx the day after that and went into it as soon as I unpacked it. Greg had two email addresses, like most of us. Both were on his laptop—his firm email address and his home, private address. The firm emails on the laptop were what I expected, with a bit of surprise. I noticed a number of clients wanting to cash out their accounts and later bitching about not getting their money promptly. Eventually the money must have been paid, however. The private emails were even more caustic, at the same time complimenting Greg on his returns and complaining that they were not getting timely quarterly distributions. I wasn't sure whether the emails were normal or not. Seeing the huge volume of emails led me to wonder what was on his cell phone. I bet it held a bunch of texts and voice mails, and the apps on his phone would reveal any other modes of communication, such as Facebook. I needed to find out from Carnegie where that was.

I had a brainstorm. I called Kurt Cousins, my go-to computer fixer in Blanco. "Hey, Kurt, I have a project for you."

"I was hoping that a rich lawyer would call me to lay money on me."

I laughed. "It's not that romantic and I'm not rich. I know you've followed the Robertson death, now a murder. I have Greg's laptop, but I know that the authorities will want it back. Is there a way you can copy and transfer everything that's on his computer onto another one?"

"Sure can. Is it an Apple or another brand?"

"It's a Dell."

"I have an old Dell I repaired and souped up. I'll sell it to you as a part of the deal and transfer everything onto that one. Should be five hundred all told."

"Good. I'll drop it off today but will need both back day after tomorrow. Don't tell anyone I did this, because I know that the FBI would not want the laptop out of my possession."

"Sure, but I'd bet that they've already done the same thing."

# 5.

PK called, mad as a wet hen. "Those guys tell me a different story every time I talk to them. At one point they told me that Goliath would never move the pipeline route forty feet to the old pipeline path that had been abandoned, and then they told me that they'd take a serious look at moving it when I sent them a possible route change that didn't interfere with other landowners. Then I heard nothing for a month. Next they came out and surveyed the plot of the original route and suggested what they called a 'flip.' This pipeline is a big one, forty-two inches. To install it, they claim they need a fifty-foot permanent easement and a temporary set of construction easements, ten feet on one side and sixty feet on the other. By flipping the big workspace to the south side, they claimed we could save a hundred of the four hundred trees they proposed to cut down and the turkey roost. I emailed them that the flip was okay with me, but I'd never heard one way or the other whether they'd move the easement south. They said they'd check. I heard nothing for a month again. When I called, they said that they figured I didn't want to agree to anything so were engineering for the original route. What assholes!"

"We need a face-to-face with someone who has decision power. That may or may not be their lawyer, who I met negotiating the city's easement. Crazy. They hired a Boston lawyer who doesn't know Texas condemnation law, but he's a sensible guy. Let me see what I can do."

• • •

"Hey, Sara. Sorry I have to bother you. How are you?"

"All right. Coping. You gave me quite a surprise telling me that Greg ordered up the codicil."

"I knew that would be the case. I wanted to update you. The FBI is involved in Greg's death now. They checked the flight logs and the Houston base station where the HondaJet was kept, and they confirmed that the plane was supposed to be fully fueled when it took off for the ranch. Someone must have drained the fuel tanks so that it wouldn't get far."

"That's terrible! Who would do that?"

"I don't have any idea, and neither does the FBI. They're starting by investigating Robertson Investments, interviewing people there, and I'm sure they'll want to talk to you."

Sara paused. "Do they know about the codicil and the reasons behind it?"

"Of course. I told them the whole story when they contacted me."

"I'm sure I'm under suspicion then."

"I don't think you'd have a clue how to get those fuel tanks drained, especially up here."

"True. Greg left everything to Chris, the pilot, to handle. The FBI should talk to him."

"You'd be smart to quietly hire a lawyer with a criminal law background to protect you. If Greg was involved in any wrongdoing, the authorities will assume that you were involved too. I've already seen people complaining in Greg's emails."

"We never talked much about the details of his business and his clients. In fact, one of the reasons you surprised me with the codicil is that we never spent a whole lot of time together except on weekends, so we didn't have time to get angry with each other. I've got a good business designing and selling high-end, customized jewelry here in Houston to the wealthy crowd. I buy diamonds mostly, but also topaz, rubies, and other stones. Only top quality. I sketch a possible piece for a client, and then once the design's set, I have a firm in San Antonio execute the piece, incorporating gems I have in inventory. The artisans are great. All Hispanic metal workers, but skilled with gold, silver and platinum. Business is so good that I have to work fifty or sixty hours a week. That's also why I rarely went to the ranch. Besides, if Greg wasn't hunting when he was there, he'd be fixated on his computer screens."

"I'll keep you up to date. Let me get to the real reason I called. I have to be in Houston to get the probate started, and I want you involved, since you have a right to any community property. You'll need a lawyer, but Ben Reeder has agreed to work with me on the probate, so you'll need to get someone else. Also, have you talked to anyone at Robertson Investments recently? Do they know I'm the executor?"

"I don't know Ben well, so I can get another lawyer. I'm sure my friends know a good lawyer. As to the people at Robertson

Investments, the only one I am close to is Rose, since we worked together a lot putting together social occasions and dinners with clients. I'm also a friend of Paul Streeter, who started the business with Greg, but I couldn't say we're close. I called him several days ago and told him what was going on."

"I take it that you have access to enough cash to keep things going for a while. As to anything you pay that is the responsibility of Greg's estate, like funeral expenses, keep a list so I can reimburse you. It'll take at least a month before the probate's filed and I'm appointed executor. Who did Greg use for his tax and other accounting needs?"

"Greg took care of that. I do remember signing a long tax return that a firm prepared. I'll take a look. The last return was two inches thick since both Greg's business and mine involve pass-through entities where everything's reported on our individual return. And yes, I have plenty of cash. Greg and I kept our businesses separate. Household expenses were paid out of a joint account we both contributed to."

"I'll call Rose and Streeter to get things started at the firm. Thanks for the information."

"What a complicated tangle this has turned out to be. And so suddenly my life's been turned upside down."

● ● ●

Probating an estate isn't really in my wheelhouse, but I've done simple probates in Blanco county a number of times. That said, I've never had to preside over such a wealthy and complicated estate. I needed help. I called Ben Reeder, the expert. Like most lawyers he didn't answer his direct line; his assistant did. I explained why I was calling. She put me through immediately. Greg's death was big news in Houston. I'd left a long voicemail and then an email with Reeder explaining the codicil and what I needed from him, and he'd replied after hours with an email saying he'd sign on as counsel for the estate. Actually, I couldn't be the lawyer for the estate since I'd been named the executor.

"Hi, John. Sorry I've been unavailable. I've been tangled up in another probate proceeding. The family is split into three different groups, and they can't agree on anything. The principal asset in the estate is an interesting company that makes robotic 'pigs' that go through pipelines to test the interior integrity of pipelines. None of them can agree on what to do with the business, but the problem is that four of the heirs and children of the heirs work at the business, and those four want to be elevated to bigger roles in the company. Selling the company is anathema, but the widow, a stepmother second wife, wants to cash out of the family. So does another sibling who doesn't work there and his children don't."

I had to chuckle. "Been there. Surprising what someone's death brings out in people."

"What can I do for you?"

"Basically take charge of the probate proceeding, starting with an engagement letter. I'm going to be relying on Greg's office and in particular his executive assistant, Rose Mendoza, to gather up whatever we will need. If you wouldn't mind, let's have a conference call with Rose and Greg's partner, Paul Streeter, to go over what we have to do and what deadlines have to be met. By the way, I've advised Sara to get a lawyer so that they can work through this with us, giving her whatever she's entitled to under community property rules."

"I'll do that. Let me get you the engagement letter and a draft of the petition for probate. Then give me two or three times that are good for you and the others."

"Deal."

The airplane crash investigator's conclusion kept returning to my mind. Setting up the crash required a high degree of sophistication and logistical support. Whoever did it had to figure out how to get to the plane without being seen. Then a fuel truck had to come into the ranch and remove the jet fuel. Where could that have gone? And without detection. An expensive operation to launch. Someone with money and resources sure had it out for Greg. Who would do such a thing?

# 6.

Next I called Streeter to set up a time for our call with Reeder and Mendoza to organize the probate process. I figured he could set things up with Rose. I got Paul immediately and explained the reason for my call.

"Things are in a tumult here, John," Streeter said. "I'll email you a few times Rose and I can get on a call. Say, technically do you represent Robertson Investments and me?"

"Not really. I'm an executor in waiting right now. What's the problem?"

"Investigators from DC are here. Not SEC regional office guys. They're auditing our records, I suppose because of client complaints regarding getting their funds returned to them promptly."

"Are the complaints legit?"

"Since you're the executor, I have to bring you into the tent. Yes, the complaints are legitimate. In fact, our liquidity has been declining for months, and the recent dip in the market due to the hostilities in the Middle East has made things worse. We had many puts and calls out there that turned worthless for clients.

They don't know that yet, and I don't know what to do. I wish Greg was still here."

"Sorry to change the subject abruptly, but who owns the firm?"

"I was employee number one after Greg and I started the firm. Greg was adamant that he didn't want to deal with other share-holders so insisted on owning everything. He promised me that I'd be compensated as if I owned twenty per cent. Over the years he made good on that promise. I'm set financially."

"Are the SEC auditors going to find anything? Who did the accounting at the firm?"

"Don't know what the auditors have found. They're pretty closed-mouth. The accounting was Greg's area. He did most of it himself but had several part-time bookkeepers outside the firm doing data entries. He even did the monthly financials. Said it was like a hobby to him."

"Who were the part-timers? Could they help us?"

"Don't know. Greg kept that as his domain. Frankly, I'm worried to death. Greg did numerous complicated trades and such with derivatives. They're designed to mimic either broad market move-ments or movements in specific indexes. They're illiquid. On top of that, his option trades in puts and calls by their nature bet on the future, and liquidating them would take away any hope of profits. We've always been short of cash because of that, so whenever a new client gave us money, instead of adding securities to the new portfolios, we turned around and gave the money to those wanting out and allocated the securities to the new money. Cash is fungible, you know."

"That leaves the firm open to charges that you guys were running a Ponzi scheme."

"Not really. Used the cash available."

"Nonetheless, what you told me sounds bad. You can count on the FBI contacting you about Greg's murder to add to the chaos over there. Back to reality, would you talk to Rose and send me the times we can get on the phone with Reeder?"

"Sure will. I wish I was hiding in the hill country with you right now."

"Hang in there. It'll take time to work through this. In the meantime, you should gather the employees and keep them in the loop, telling them that things will be all right down the road. Let them know that their jobs are safe for now."

"I sure hope so."

●  ●  ●

I actually had two cases involving Goliath. Besides PK's fight, I had a big valuation hearing involving the city of Blanco with Goliath's lawyers and representatives regarding their running the pipeline through the northern edge of the city's boundaries. They'd have to cross city streets and a small lot the city used for storage. I'd gotten a big valuation from our appraiser, and they naturally got a much smaller one. I was looking for at least a million for the city, but the real pressure on me came from another source: city residents who opposed any pipeline in the hill country. The purpose of the hearing was simply to set the damage in the value of the property caused by the pipeline being installed there. The hearing had nothing to do with the merits of the route.

I showed up early. I asked PK to be there in the hope that we could have our face-to-face with Goliath decision makers. Goliath insisted on having the hearing in San Marcos to avoid protesters, so they rented a room at a Holiday Inn Express on the outskirts of town. Their four representatives and lawyers showed up early as well. As we gathered, I pulled them away for a quick meeting with PK.

"What's the status of moving the pipeline? You guys said you'd take a serious look at that."

"I don't know," said Tom Langtry, supposedly the supervisor of the Goliath field workers. "I'll give it a try again. Let me call the route supervisor at Goliath."

"I told PK early on they wouldn't move the route," said Trey, the guy PK had worked with on the ground negotiating the route and who stood next to Langtry.

That made PK mad. "You guys told me numerous times that Goliath would seriously consider it, and you also offered the compromise of flipping the work space to avoid cutting down as many trees."

Tom intervened. "Let's see what Anna at Goliath says." He went outside onto a deck to call Goliath, talked for ten minutes, then returned. "She'll take one last full look at moving the pipeline and will get back to us."

• • •

Probating a will in Texas is streamlined and simple. In years long past, every expense and every sale of an asset had to get court approval, so heirs could see their inheritance going mostly to lawyers. Many lawyers simply charged a per cent, usually two, for each transaction in and out. A half century ago, however, the legislature reformed the probate law because there was little benefit served by requiring court approvals of everything. Now, the judge simply qualifies the executor, making sure he is who he says he is and that he's not disqualified. Then the judge empowers the executor to gather the assets, pay any liabilities, file an inventory of the assets and liabilities, pay any bills, and finally make the distributions directed by the will. After the judge reviews what's been accomplished by the executor, he closes the estate and discharges the executor.

Sounds simple, and in most cases it is. For Greg Robertson's estate, this probate promised to be the reverse. I hoped that Rose could save me time and trouble gathering up records of the things that Greg owned besides his firm, figure out who he owed for what, and help me obtain values for each significant asset. Didn't look like the HondaJet accident would lead to a lawsuit, at least against the manufacturer. Then there was the firm. With an SEC cloud hanging over it, no telling what that asset was worth. Maybe nothing. I couldn't see how I could possibly close up his estate until the aircraft crash was solved. Maybe the base operator in Houston shorted the refueling. More likely, someone had it in for Greg. Then I had to figure out what property was community and what separate so that Sara and the estate could agree to a fair division. I was waiting for a reaction from Sara pushing back on the ownership issue. Now, instead of sitting in my position as executor, she was a widow under suspicion with no control over the firm or the future.

I called Stonewater to start off my Monday morning. The weekend had given me two days to unwind from the stress over PK's pipeline fight and the loose ends with the Robertsons and their businesses.

"Good morning, Oliver."

"Hi John. Calling for an update?"

"Not really. More to bring you up to date on a few things. In looking into the laptop, it occurred to me that Greg's cell phone must hold additional information that could help both of us. Did the NTSB turn it over to you?"

"Nope. Good idea. Do you have the password for that?"

"I'll get it from Rose or Sara."

"What else? I'm pretty busy here," Oliver said

"Have you talked to the SEC?"

"They haven't called. Why would they?"

"They'll add another layer of concern to you. The initial investigation they're doing makes me think that the firm is in financial trouble and perhaps operating what could look like a Ponzi scheme, using new investor money to fund old investor distributions and redemptions."

"Not sure that any of the wealthy people he dealt with would get mad enough to get involved in a scheme to murder Greg."

"No telling. I don't want to tell you your business, but your guys might want to review the investor list, especially the ones who filed complaints against the company," I awkwardly commented.

"You're right. Send me the contact information for the SEC investigators involved with the firm. Right now, as you can tell, we don't have any leads pointing to who's responsible for the murder."

"Now let me bring you up to date on a few things. We talked to Chris Morgan, the pilot, and he confirmed that after the last flight, he had the base operator refuel the aircraft. The aircraft wasn't flown after that until Greg flew it to the ranch. That led us to the manager of the base operator where the plane was hangered, and they confirmed the refuel. They said the plane was in good shape, that HondaJet people came to the hanger to do a checkup and maintenance two weeks before Greg flew there. Then we talked to David Steward, known as I4U2. Not much there either. Surly son of a bitch. We wanted to see if he had any connection to the murder since he was a customer of Sara and had an identical plane in the same hanger. He wouldn't tell us anything other than to deny he had anything to do with Greg and his plane. He did ask why the plane crashed, and I told him that was not my bailiwick, that he should contact the NTSB."

"Thanks for the update," Oliver said

"You're welcome. Bye for now."

# 7.

More trouble. Sara called. "I can't believe all these things bubbling up at once. Can you recommend a Houston lawyer to me?"

"A probate attorney?"

"That too, but I think I need a criminal defense lawyer right now."

"Why?"

"An FBI agent named Stonewater interviewed me yesterday at his office. He wanted to discuss the circumstances regarding Greg's death. He read me something called my Miranda rights, but since I haven't done anything, I went ahead with the interview. I don't think he learned anything important about Greg's death, but he did hone in on my jewelry business and especially where I bought stones. Then this morning he called to tell me that Paragon Diamonds, the firm I buy my diamonds from in New York city, was on their watch list because they had been caught selling unregistered diamonds. He called them blood diamonds."

"What are they?"

"He says blood diamonds are from mainly African countries where there's fighting going on. He said rebels force locals to mine diamonds, and then the raw diamonds are sold on the black market and find their way to underground diamond cutters in Belgium. Then the diamonds are smuggled into JFK with the help of ground crews. The diamonds never get registered with the diamond registry called the Kimberley Process, an international diamond registry formed to control that kind of trade and, he said, he thought to control the supply of diamonds world-wide to keep the prices up. The Canadians have their own certification process. I don't have any certificates for my diamonds."

"Do you think your diamonds are unregistered?"

"According to Stonewater, I'm the ideal conduit for blood diamonds, since my business is off the radar of the big companies. He said that there's a ten per cent tariff on polished diamonds, and importation of blood diamonds has been banned by executive order since 2007. I doubt I'm involved in any kind of illegal activity. I don't know though. I bought my stones from Paragon since they're such high quality and less expensive than going to one of the big diamond houses."

"Did Greg know Paragon Diamond's business or people well, how they did in the diamond trade?"

"That's where it gets sticky. Greg travelled to New York frequently to meet with clients and his investment banker friends, and three or four times I had him pick up stones from Paragon to bring home in the HondaJet. So Paragon knew him, but I don't think Greg ever gave a thought to where the diamonds came from."

"Interesting. What else did Stonewater ask you?"

"Nothing that surprised me. He delved into our relationship, and I told him the troubles we had in our relationship. One thing I didn't tell you before has to do with Greg's social habits. He had two close relationships with senior female analysts at Goldman and JP Morgan. I wasn't ever sure anything went on with them, but every month Greg went to confabs, usually in New York, focused on one industry or another. Greg freely mentioned being with them, you know, dining with them and such. I never suspected anything until our physical relationship dried up. Who knows? Sorry to dump this on you."

"Did you tell Stonewater your suspicions?"

"Sure. I didn't want to hold back. We had our problems, but divorce was not an alternative when Greg died."

"I'll email the contact information for Bob Rivera. He's a long-time friend of mine and practices criminal defense law exclusively. I'll also send you the names of a couple of probate and estate planning lawyers to represent you in Greg's probate to make sure I divide things up the right way. And you'll want to look at your will and change it in light of Greg's death."

"I'll be up to my ears in lawyers. Can I continue my jewelry business?"

"I have no idea and shouldn't be giving you advice, but I sure wouldn't be buying any more stones from Paragon right now."

That elicited a short laugh from Sara. "Got ya."

I knew how Sara felt, a bit overwhelmed with so many moving parts in the Robertson world. I was too.

• • •

My conversation with Sara reminded me to find out where Greg's cell phone was. I'd gotten the password from her earlier but didn't know where the phone actually was. I called Carnegie at the NTSB.

"Hi John."

"I won't take up much of your time today. I'm only calling to find out where Greg's cell phone is."

"We sent it to Stonewater yesterday, and he should have it today, along with a transcript of the emails and voicemails on it. Nothing relevant to the airplane incident, so I don't need it back. He'll need it. Pretty surprising stuff."

"Anything to indicate who might have been after him physically?"

"Not really. Based on what's in the transcript, I think you should get an outside accounting firm to do a forensic study on the firm to make sure the accounting is accurate."

"Will do."

Right after Carnegie's call, I called my friend Rivera to give him a heads up that Sara would be calling. His reaction was typical.

"I wish she hadn't said anything to the authorities before she talked to me. I'll give her a call today even though the first call is supposed to be the client calling the lawyer. The diamond business concerns me. Innocent people sometime get caught up in illegal business thinking they're getting a special deal. A quarter of my business involves clients being charged with possessing stolen property, usually motor cycles and ag equipment. The diamonds introduce an international flavor to this, and DeBeers and the others are rabid trying to stamp out the blood diamond trade. May be a criminal violation to import blood diamonds, especially if the ten per cent duty wasn't paid on them. She's not a part of that though. An innocent purchaser. I'll keep you up to date best I can since Sara will be my client, not you."

"I understand. Thanks. I've got a question, though. You might not want to answer. Let's assume that one of Greg's clients, or even Sara, got totally pissed at Greg. There are angry emails and voice mails from clients demanding money. If one of them wanted to do Greg in by orchestrating an airplane crash, could any of them, assuming they're upright citizens, find somebody to do the dirty deed?"

Bob paused. "I hang around with the worst of the worst, defending them for big bucks. The low level guys aren't capable of pulling off sophisticated operations like that. Most haven't ever flown in an aircraft. To arrange that, you'd have to go to the upper levels of those involved in the drug trade. They'll do anything for the right price."

"How would a rich guy get in touch with someone like that?"

"You can never tell. Remember Carroll Johnson, the oil and gas guy who did drugs and later killed himself?"

"Yep. A good reminder that people who do drugs interact with bad people. Dangerous people. Time'll tell." We said our good-byes. Bob was always interesting. He lived in a different world than mine. Maybe not the Robertsons though. I thought about I4U2 and his friends.

I called Paul Streeter, next on my list. At least I could work in the hills as long as I had my phone and a good internet connection. The early March morning was simply beautiful, warmer than usual at seventy-five, and not a cloud in the sky. I moved my work to the back porch. "Hey, Paul. How are you doing with the SEC breathing down your neck?"

"Not so well. They look grim and said they'd be wrapping things up in less than a week. Not a word what they might have found or what they're thinking."

"That's standard procedure, but the reason I'm calling is to ask you to call Rob Hall, a friend of mine, and get him and his firm to do a quick audit of the books so that we can find out where our vulnerabilities are. I'll send him a copy of what's on Greg's laptop."

Streeter paused, obviously nervous from so many outsiders poking around the firm. "I'll call him right away. Is he representing the firm or you or who?"

"Not sure. The estate as the owner of the firm."

"Will Hall and you be open with me and the others here? I don't like how the SEC people don't tell us anything. If they found something wrong, I might be able to explain what was going on."

" Rob and I will keep you in the loop. Is anything in particular worrying you?"

"No. I saw Greg doing weird things from time to time."

"Let's get Rob involved and tell him that I'll be coming to Houston a week from now. We could meet Monday in the afternoon."

"Okay."

That night, I realized that I needed to get myself a retainer and do the same for Ben Reeder, Rob and anyone else providing services, given the financial stress on both Robertson Investments and the estate. I attended to that the next morning. I also needed to check in with Stonewater. I knew that at some point he'd clam up on me, since investigations are private. As executor I had to figure out where Greg's money should go and certainly didn't want to give any to any beneficiary involved in the murder. If Greg had been involved in financial wrongdoing, before I could distribute any money or close the estate I'd have to address any liabilities stemming from the irregularities.

"Hi, John. Any news from your end?" Stonewater greeted me. I briefed him on the SEC investigation and our retaining an outside auditor.

"I've got the cell for you but it has to be on loan for you to look at and return to me. I don't want anything erased, even though the NTSB transcribed the voice mails and listed the calls in and out. I'll make a copy for you. I think you'll be surprised. I've turned over the information to the SEC so we can coordinate our investigations."

"So what will surprise me?"

"For starters, it's a treasure trove of contacts, emails, voice-mails and notes. Your concerns are right on. Seems Robertson was juggling money right and left, and unbeknownst to people at the firm or at the SEC, he borrowed a cool million from his bank to shore up the company's finances. On the books he showed the money as a capital contribution, but the loan's a joint loan of his personally and of his firm. That's a technical reporting viola-tion according to my SEC friends. I'm told that financial guys like Robertson use their cell phones rather than landlines at the office to make calls and have conversations that regulators can't listen in to. Robertson didn't use a burner phone as far as we know, so we might find something from the voice mails and from call records if we subpoena them. It's all there.

"You should also focus on the calls and voice mails from Sal Minardi. He's connected somehow with Paragon Diamonds, the company Sara bought diamonds from. Looks like Greg got him or Paragon to invest through Robertson Investments. Over the past year the investments have been substantial, like low eight figures.

I'll let you listen to the angry voice mails and see the emails for yourself. Sal wasn't happy. He kept demanding information about Robertson's firm and his accounts at the firm. Look at the one on February 27; Sal for the first time sounded threatening. Said his principals would be out for blood. Our first lead."

"Good grief. I'll take a look. Thanks."

# 8.

I'd moved to Blanco fifteen years ago to have a more relaxed lifestyle, avoiding the high pressure, big-dollar engagements that had allowed me the luxury of buying my perfectly sized, one-hundred-acre ranch. Meeting Carla and marrying her later anchored our being here. And then with three kids joining us, two of them fosters, the small but excellent public schools attracted us. Remaining in Blanco couldn't be questioned. My only problem was my current schedule. PK's pipeline litigation, the Robertson probate with its complexities, my city attorney obligations and piles of the usual disputes and documents kept me working sixty hours a week. Not the plan.

I decided to work from home for a while. That way Carla and I could visit between projects. I called Tom Langtry to check on Goliath's willingness to move the pipeline.

"Nothing to report. We're running out of time. The original route is still the standard so we have no alternative but to go ahead."

"What did Anna say?"

"Haven't heard from her," Langtry said casually.

Now I started steaming after telling PK to cool it. "Look, Tom, we need answers. If nothing else works we want you to flip the work space."

"The bottom line is that Goliath ain't gonna move the route. They don't do that. And the flip can only happen if we get PK and the other five landowners along the line from the road to the eastern end of his property to consent to the flip."

"Send me the papers for that right away. I'm sure PK can get that done." I was angry. I felt as if PK and I were the grass, and the elephant was grinding us down and winning. I called PK and told him where we were.

"Good to see my lawyer finally riled up," PK said. "They don't care about us landowners. They want to get their job done, and the easiest way to do that is to turn everything into a money issue. They can't handle people like us who won't accept a payoff. So here I am, facing either a hundred and twenty foot swath through my trees with no easement agreement and no money, litigating the money for three years, or submitting to them, getting the flip done best we can, and taking the money. I'll use a quarter of the money replanting trees in the work zones they've cleared. I want this punishment over with and know that I can't fight the pipelines. The law gives them almost unlimited power, and they have deep money pockets I can't keep up with."

"Shouldn't they be the ones getting the landowners along the line to consent?"

"Theoretically, yes, but I've talked to most of them, and they're so pissed at Goliath that they'd refuse to do anything they asked for. They'll work with me once I explain what's at stake though."

"Painful. Reminds me of Kenny Rogers song about knowing when to hold 'em and when to fold 'em."

"Send the papers on when you get them."

Not a happy way to start my day, and ugly things came to dominate the day.

● ● ●

Next on my list was finding out where we were with Robertson Investments. I called Rob Hall to find out what he had turned up. Streeter had confirmed earlier that he'd retained Rob right after I suggested he do that.

"Hi, John. You've got quite a big set of problems here in Houston."

"What do you mean?"

"We've looked through the laptop and the firm's records, but we also verified assets and checked with banks and the counter-parties involved in the shorts, puts and calls. What's on the firm's servers and what's on Greg's laptop are different. In reviewing his laptop's contents, we discovered that Greg executed naked shorts, that is, short sales without providing the shares to back the short up. Not supposed to do that. When the market zoomed up on the good news that China and the US had reached a trade agreement, his position got called and he had to cover. Cost him over seven figures. To add to that, the amount he lost on puts wiped out his profits on his calls. Then there's the problem with his clients. The records and emails show that many clients wanted to get their money back because of the volatility right now and because they sensed Greg was losing big money."

"What's the balance sheet look like right now?"

"Not good. I'd guess that there're a number of unrecorded liabilities out there, and if they were recorded the firm would be bankrupt. Still need to finish investigating that. The emails on the laptop, for instance, show there were financial dealings with the Bank of America, but there aren't any assets or liabilities on the firm's balance sheet showing anything from that bank."

"If there are shortages in the clients' accounts, aren't they covered by the federal insurance on customer accounts?"

"Sure, for the money in their accounts, but not the losses from trading."

"Hmmm. How many mad clients are out there?"

"Over forty. That's another mystery. Two big accounts are listed as anonymous LLCs. The employer ID numbers we checked were bogus. Nothing in the records to show who owns the accounts. We only know that the money originally came from JPMorgan. I'm sure we'll clear that up as soon as the news of the firm's distress becomes public.

"But I haven't told you the worst. We've found two sets of accounts for the clients on Greg's laptop. The first one must have been the one he furnished clients, showing a number of transactions, nearly all profitable. The format for each individual account statement sent to clients duplicated the others except for the amounts involved. Greg created a second, separate file folder showing the actual balances of the client accounts. Every account has major cumulative losses. A month before he died he stopped updating any of the accounts. That coincided with the troubles in the Mideast, and I understand from Streeter that major losses were incurred. I've had to turn the information over to the SEC, and I'm sure they'll shut Robertson Investments down in the next day or two."

"Would you send me any information you have on any accounts that Greg or Sara had at the firm? That'll impact the probate for sure. And I'll have to pen in the firm value at zero. I hope it's not a liability for the estate."

"Agreed. I'll send a bill so I can financially keep ahead."

"Good. I'll get it paid."

Time for a break. Already eleven. I made coffee, took fresh bagels out of the fridge to toast and coaxed Carla to take time off to sit in the gazebo by our pond, that is, our "tanque", and de-stress. A beautiful morning, with a light breeze blowing across the gazebo. I brought Carla up to date, in part to see what she'd say. Her intuition always worked well, and since I had none to speak of, I valued her reactions.

"Seems to me, John, that the core issue is who did Greg in. Could Greg have committed suicide, knowing where things were headed at the firm?"

That struck me like a lightning bolt. Hadn't even occurred to me. "The outside factors sure could lead to that kind of suspicion, but knowing Greg the optimist, I don't think that was on his agenda. I still think somebody killed him."

"Let's see," Carla said. "Sara is a suspect since she and Greg were having trouble and Sara suspected Greg of having relation-ships with other women. However, killing Greg was a sophisticated operation made to look like an accident, and I've not heard that you have any indication that she knew anyone who could pull that off. Not her anyway. Then there are the clients of Greg's firm. Rob thinks that the client losses are in the millions since he handled over a billion in client funds.

"Years ago, I followed the Bernard Madoff scandal in New York, and he lost millions for his clients too. Even those who got out early had to cough up any profits. Many mad people, but nothing violent as far as I know. Then there is Paragon, the diamond merchants. Their possibly dealing in blood diamonds doesn't have anything to do with Greg, and Sara buying from them is no basis for them being violent with her husband. On the other hand, if Paragon had invested money with Greg, they might have had a motive. However, if you had big money with Greg and wanted him to give it back, you wouldn't kill him. That would mean you'd never get your money back. Still no one out there to name as a suspect."

"That's correct," I said. "Let's see what comes of this."

"I know you're the executor for Greg's estate, but please, please, don't get involved like you're a detective. You've done that too many times, and I don't want you threatened, much less the kids and me."

"I hear you. I'll try to sort out Robertson Investments. That one'll be difficult but I will have help. I'm hoping the bad financial situation doesn't spread to the estate. There are complaints out there that might make the estate liable. The Madoff family members had to turn over the money they'd made even though they claimed they didn't know what Bernie was doing."

"Don't let it stress you. As the old saying goes, 'I didn't do it and I can't fix it. End of story.'"

"True, but there will be plenty of mad people out there, and with Greg gone, I'll be the one being blamed."

# 9.

I'd been avoiding going to Houston, but the time had come. Over time I'd become allergic to big cities. The official court appointment of me as executor was at hand, so Sunday early evening I trekked to Houston and checked in at the Lancaster Hotel, conveniently across the street from the Texas Tower. Their restaurant was not five stars. As I gorged on a hamburger and fries, the thought occurred to me that I might be representing not only a bankrupt investment firm but a bankrupt estate. After overeating and worrying about the Robertson estate's affairs, I tossed and turned most of the night.

At least the morning weather cooperated, although for early March the temperature was a bit chilly. Ben and I met at the probate court, which along with the family courts, was ensconced in a poorly maintained, old building that the civil courts called an annex. Only the important civil and criminal cases are heard in the nice old court house. My appointment turned out to be the same non-event that I had presided over as the attorney for estates in Blanco. The judge called my name, and I gave his clerk my driver's license, the original will, and a death certificate. The judge admonished me to act reasonably, do what Greg's will instructed me to do and then signed the order. Took less than ten minutes once my name came up. Ben excused himself, and I went off to the Robertson Investments office.

I'd arranged for Rob to meet me there in the conference room to hear in more detail what he had to say about the state of the firm's finances. Rob had already arrived by eleven, the appointed hour. More quiet than usual. Paul Streeter and Rose came into the conference room as I strode in; I suppose the receptionist told them I'd arrived. Their presence made Rob uneasy, but I figured if he had bad news I'd need allies on the ground to work through the problems Rob had warned me about. I told Rob to go ahead and explained why the other two were to stay in the room.

"I haven't done a forensic audit in a while, but here's the bottom line: the official books on your server don't reflect the truth," Rob began. "Thanks for the extra laptop you duplicated. His records contain two sets of books, the one you have and the real one he kept to himself. That secret file was password protected, but thankfully he used one that Sara had given to you. We also found a number of 'off the books' transactions by checking the banks that Greg did business with, both through the firm and personally. No one questioned his authority, so when he needed money, he drew down on an unsecured line of credit he'd established at Bank of America. From what I can tell, he used the accounts there to send refunds to clients who were giving him trouble for not paying them off earlier. He then juggled the books to show the client's account paid off. Greg hadn't told his clients that they'd been losing money, so what he paid and what the account really was often differed substantially. Over three months the difference between the artificial accounts and the real accounts at the firm ballooned to over a negative ten million, and borrowing on the line of credit to cover the losses hit the max. Greg never entered the Bank of America line of credit as a firm liability. I think Greg eventually simply ran out of ammunition. I'm sure he thought his fortunes would change and his investments would appreciate and get him out of the box, but once the markets stabilized, they went flat, preventing Greg from recouping his losses. Not sure what Greg then intended to do, but he kept robbing Peter to pay Paul. I've reported all this to the SEC. Legally obligated to do that. Here's a balance sheet I have drafted to show what I think is the true state of affairs. Robertson Investments itself has a negative net worth of around seventeen million, believe it or not, once the Bank of America loan is booked and losses in the investments are properly reflected. The fact that he used incoming investment funds to pay off disgruntled investors makes matters worse. I can show you on Greg's laptop how he kept the two sets of books."

The room was silent. Greg's personal involvement in the accounting machinations and deceptions meant that the estate would be on the hook for the firm's losses to clients. Glad I had taken out a retainer and got one to Rob before this came to light. And what Rob told us meant that suicide might have been the case.

As we broke up the meeting, Rose came over quietly and asked to talk to me. "I'd like to go over several things you don't know about Greg. Do you have time?"

Intrigued, I said "Sure. Let's get lunch downstairs."

The closest real restaurant was in the tunnel system, Molina's Mexican Restaurant. Since it was late, we had no problem getting a table. Rose started. "There are several facts you need to know about. First, in late December last year, Greg took out a jumbo life insurance policy for six million dollars. Like your codicil, the beneficiaries are not what you'd expect. Greg's two brothers and Sara are named equal beneficiaries. Sara must not have told you, but that's what started the split between the two of them. She found out about the policy because she was interviewed as a part of the application. She didn't want Greg spending their money on his brothers, even as beneficiaries. Then she and Greg got into a fight over who owned what. Greg argued that the ranch was his separate property, and Sara argued otherwise. Sad to see two nice people like that get into fights over money. Frankly, I think they were headed for a divorce. Besides the money, Greg loved women. Not me. I'm married and made that clear to him early on. But I did his expense reports and often saw strange charges, like flowers, gifts and once in a while double bookings at hotels. Part of my job was not to ask questions."

"You know Sara. This is hard for me to even ask. Could she have been so angry that she arranged his death?"

"I don't know. I don't think so, but I do know that she dealt with odd characters in her jewelry business. The weirdest ones were a group of rappers who fawned over her and her jewelry. I4U2 is their leader, and Sara met him when they were each both at the hanger going on a trip. One of the gang even got killed in a knife fight last month. Greg didn't want her dealing with low-lives, and Sara didn't want Greg's pilot farmed out to I4U2 or his ilk."

"Anything else?" I asked as we chowed down on excellent enchiladas.

"Not really. I'll send you a list of assets I've put together, along with that balance sheet you gave me and found on his laptop. I made footnotes on each balance sheet asset listed and expanded what I thought each one was. I didn't address the liabilities."

"The Robertsons and their lives get more complicated as I dig into this. Thank you for being so open and thorough putting the information together. I'm afraid this will get worse before it gets better."

"I'm happy that we can work together and talk freely. My husband's tired of hearing my complaints and fears."

"All we can do is take one step forward at a time. We'll see where we end up." Rose and I said our goodbyes, quite full from lunch.

I limped back to Blanco that afternoon. On the way I brought Carla up to date and then called Stonewater. He didn't act as if the state of affairs at Robertson Investments surprised him, and of course he wanted to talk immediately to Rob. He added that he'd get a team together to interview the staff at the firm, particularly Rose and Paul, to find out what and when they knew that Greg had suffered financial reverses and began to cover them up. Too bad I only learned the truth after I'd been appointed executor. Otherwise I would have declined the appointment and let Greg's brothers untangle everything.

• • •

Bob Rivera, my friend whom I recommended to Sara to defend her, called. "John, I'm calling to thank you for referring Sara Robertson to me. The ideal client. Plenty of money and plenty of trouble." You have to have a sense of humor to be in criminal defense.

"Glad to have you aboard. Later you'll want a briefing on the estate and Greg's firm. Complex and numerous facts. All negative."

"As with life. Smart and sophisticated as she is, I can't see her arranging to kill her husband. Way out of any skill sets she has. Her real problem is her diamond jewelry business. Not sure what happens to diamonds if they were illegally smuggled into the country. I even thought of a potential disaster. If Customs tried to confiscate the blood diamonds that Sara put into her customers' jewelry, havoc would result and kill her business."

"Goal one is to find out whether Greg committed suicide or whether he was killed by someone else. I'd agree that Sara is an unlikely murderess. Naturally she denies doing him in. But with the money she has, she could have hired the job out to someone."

"They all say that they didn't do it. I never ask though. But please keep me up to date on any information you get about the murder or suicide, whatever."

"Sure will. Next time I'm in Houston, let's get together for a drink and tell lies to each other."

"Sounds like fun."

I thought that Greg's death wouldn't be explained until someone figured out why and how his aircraft went down. Stonewater might have news, so I called. "Glad you called. A bit of news. Complicated though. You know that one reason aircraft are so expensive is that every little piece has to have an ID number so that each item can be traced in the event of what the FAA calls an 'incident'. When the NTSB took the plane apart, they went into the electronics. The flight deck on that plane is high state-of-the-art.

Mostly visual with computer screens. Like cars these days, behind the screens are computers and modules that address each aspect shown on the flight deck screens. The NTSB pulled the module that measures fuel levels and found that the module was not the original. The module was genuine, mind you, but whatever was in there was not the one originally in the plane. My guys contacted HondaJet, and of course they were more than cooperative, since they want to make sure that the plane didn't go down because of a defect. This morning they called back to tell me that the module in the plane had been purchased in Zurich by an aircraft maintenance company, and that company said it had sold it to a company in Serbia that they'd never heard of. We'll be trying to identify that entity but I'm sure we'll hit a dead end. Carnegie said he sent the module to its lab in DC to pull down the firmware and software to analyze it. HondaJet gave them a new module to use as a comparison."

"I'm surprised. Anyone this sophisticated has to have big money to pull off an 'accident' like this."

"Not sure who we're pursuing. Sara couldn't have done it alone. Rich people who gave money to Robertson are usually not the kind of people inclined to get involved in criminal activity. I'll let you know if anything else pops up."

• • •

On my way home that evening, as I turned off highway 32 onto Cambridge Road toward my house, I saw a white nameless pickup parked on the side of the road. Unusual, but it could have been a monitor for the electric company, or even a pipeline contractor.

Since more and more people pull off to take cellphone calls, I dismissed it being there. But Greg's unsolved death made me wonder if the man in the car was somehow involved in that. I didn't mention it to Carla when I brought her up to date on the module.

"I'm afraid. What are you going to do about Robertson Investments?"

"I've been thinking. The financial tangle at the firm is too big and too technical for me to handle. Rob says the firm has a huge negative net worth, so the only thing to do is to file it in bankruptcy. That'll take experienced bankruptcy attorneys, but the filing will relieve me of having to sort out the machinations that have gone on there. The SEC will close the firm down anyway. I'm afraid that what Greg did will make his estate liable, and his assets will be stripped away by the bankruptcy attorney."

"I'm glad you're going to do that. You don't need the stress, and whoever is front and center in the bankruptcy will be cursed and yelled at by the investors who lost money. I've been wondering. Did Greg ever study the innards of his airplane? How it worked, was maintained, that sort of thing."

"Interesting question. My eyes glazed over when Greg told me the details of his neat little commuter jet. He was really into it. Even got a commercial pilot's license, but I doubt whether he knew what the techie pieces behind the flight deck screens were."

"Okay. Given that you know that the firm was in trouble financially, suicide looks like a real possibility. That'll complicate your handling the estate, especially the insurance policy."

*Too many variables popping up with Robertson. Time to call my friend Hal Shaw. Hal retired from the FBI a long while ago, but he's kept his edge. I needed someone to whom I could dump all* the data I had in my head to help me understand what had gone on and then figure out where events were headed. In particular I couldn't solve who was behind Greg's death, even if it was Greg himself.

I called Hal and briefed him on what I knew. "Thanks for calling. You've got my juices going again. Several things are clear to me. First, of course, is that Greg's death was intentional, but the signs are mixed whether his death was a suicide or whether he was murdered. On the one hand, Greg could have staged this to make his death look like an accident. As you know, a life insurance policy becomes incontestable after a year, but the policy was not that old, so the insurance company's going to be motivated to claim the accident was a rigged suicide. On the other hand, given the state of Robertson Investments, I'd bet there are enough investors who are totally pissed. One of them may have had it in for Greg and didn't care that killing him might make things worse. Might make things better for them, come to think of it. I'd focus on the investor list."

"Thanks, Hal. Good thoughts. I'll look into the investors. My next task is to get a firm in Houston to file a bankruptcy for Greg's company. That'll smoke out who the investors are and whether any of them are candidates for orchestrating the crash."

# 10.

The next morning I went to my office and called Grainger and Grainger, a Houston firm specializing in bankruptcies. Better for the moment that Carla didn't hear the ugly facts I had to lay out. I told my story to three or four lawyers, and they agreed to handle the matter. One of those was a mid-level partner, Susan Becker. Took over two hours of back and forth even though I told them that Rob, Rose and Paul would give them the information they'd need for the filing.

They suggested a Chapter 11 proceeding, in which the company could continue to remain in control, continue operating and work toward an orderly liquidation. I told the lawyers that they had to make that decision, but since the company was in such a deep hole and misconduct appeared to be the reason for the bankruptcy, a simple Chapter 7 full bankruptcy and liquidation managed by an independent trustee might be fairer to all the parties. I suspected they'd want to avoid that since it would limit their fees severely. I wanted out of this, so I left the decision to them. And with that I handed Robertson Investments' fate over to Susan Becker and the other lawyers at Grainger and Granger.

I still had Greg's estate to handle. I decided not to call Rose to see what information she had regarding Greg's personal financial affairs, given the turmoil that had to be going on at Robertson Investments. I had to start somewhere. Rose's list of assets helped, but her information didn't include any liabilities other than Greg's expense account items that the firm was supposed to reimburse him for. The out of date personal balance sheet and income statement on Greg's laptop helped. He'd dated it the November 30st, just prior to his loan at Bank of America. He must have used that to get his loan. Nothing surprising. He'd put most of his money, except what he'd need for personal expenses, into accounts at the firm. I knew those accounts would be frozen, so I turned to the usual assets—home, car, clothes and personal effects—and the ranch, which I assumed was his separate property. Greg had mentioned that he kept a ranch operating account at the Texas Regional Bank, so before I called Rose to go over what she had sent me, I called on my friend Judy at the bank. The bank's across the street from my courthouse office.

"Hi, John. I bet you're up to your ears in the Robertson death and the pipeline fights!"

"Sure am. I knew you'd need this, but here's a copy of my appointment as executor of Greg's estate. I'm here to get things started and need to know what the balance in the ranch's operating account was on his date of death. Need to get the current balance as well."

"Let me see," she said as she swiveled over to her computer. "He died on April 10, didn't he?"

"Yep."

"The balance was $14,523.97 at the end of that day. Looks like the account received an auto-deposit of $10,000 a month from somewhere. The balance today is $16,342.53. It's an interest-bearing account for what that's worth."

"Good. Thanks."

"You do know that Mr. Robertson kept a safety deposit box here too, right?"

I was surprised. "No, I didn't. Wonder what he needed that for. Can you open it up for me?"

"No can do. Sorry. We need his key to get into it or a court order to drill the lock."

"Damn. I understand. I'll see what he had in his office here. Have to do that anyway. I'll need access to that operating account. Who signs checks on that account besides Greg?"

"Let's see. Greg, a person named Rose Mendoza, and Gary Servring. Robertson was the only signatory on the safety deposit box. Gary's his ranch manager. I've known him since he was a kid. Good guy."

"Great. Thanks. I'll be in touch."

Nothing's easy sorting out the facts when you can't talk to someone who's died. I called Servring. "Gary, I don't think we've been introduced but I'm Greg's executor. Can I come out and look over Greg's office and see what information I can find related to the probate of his estate? In particular, I'm looking for a key to his safety deposit box at the bank here."

"Sure. Come on. Didn't spend any time to speak of in his office. Didn't need to. Greg liked to discuss ranch matters over coffee in the kitchen, and the checkbook's in the ranch office at the barn."

Not having any hearings or appointments that morning, I drove out to the ranch and Greg's mansion. How transitory life is. I remembered learning the phrase "Sic transit gloria mundi" in my high school Latin class in Houston. "So passes worldly glory." Nothing lasts. I wondered who would clean up things when I died. Probably Carla. That reminded me that I needed to let her know everything and keep a record of where everything was. Especially my passwords.

I knocked on the front door, and a pleasant middle-aged Hispanic woman answered. Since no one can get into the ranch without knowing the gate passcode, she didn't seem particularly apprehensive.

"Good morning, Mr. Mariner. I'm Lorena. Gary told me you'd be out here this morning."

"Good to meet you." I explained what I had come for.

"I remember your being out here several times. I think Mr. Robertson showed you his office, so let's start there. Come with me."

To my surprise, his office was locked, but Lorena had a key. "Mr. Robertson gave this key to me so that I could clean his office, but he told me never to let anyone into the office without his permission. I guess it's okay for us to go in now."

Lorena stood by as I went through Greg's desk and file drawer. Oddly, the computer screens were full on. No one had thought to turn them off, so I did. Nothing much in the way of files since, I assumed, the business records that didn't relate to the ranch were either on his laptop or in his office in Houston. Thankfully, in the middle drawer of his desk, in a separate little section I found what looked like the safety deposit key in a small envelope with the bank logo on it. The bank statements were in the bottom right drawer, many unopened. Greg didn't keep a close eye on the money going in and out at the ranch, trusting Gary.

Being curious why Greg might need a safety deposit box, I went back to have Judy open it for me. In front of the small area set aside for the safety deposit boxes was an amusing sign that said the bank wasn't responsible for anything related to the boxes. If there was a break-in at the bank and the robbers took valuables out of the boxes, the owners would be out of luck. Judy took her key and I took mine, we opened the little door, and she handed me the box, motioning me over to the table in the back corner of the room where the safety deposit boxes were. Then she left the room.

I opened the box expecting to see papers relating to the ranch, mainly the deed and title insurance policy. When I opened it, the box was half filled with small plastic bags, a quarter of the size of sandwich bags, with closures. Each had a logo of Paragon Diamonds on it, and each contained a clear diamond. There were various markings on small tabs on each bag, with four notations— carat, color, clarity and cut. Each bag had each category filled in. The diamonds were white and three or four carats. Various cuts. Under clarity, most had "VVS1" or "VVS2", but several had "IF". I had no idea what those things meant, but there were seventeen bags total. Nothing else in the box. Nothing. I didn't know what those diamonds were worth, but I knew I'd found a major asset. Made the one carat diamond Carla and I bought when we got married look tiny. I made a list of each diamond, put each of them back in the box, and then put the box back into its receptacle. I went back to my office wondering why Greg had bought the diamonds and then hid them here in Blanco.

I wondered whether the diamonds were Sara's. I called her.

"Sara, I wondered whether Greg ever bought diamonds for you to keep here in the hills."

"No. By the way, thanks for the referral to Bob Rivera. I feel much better. What are you talking about?"

"I discovered a safety deposit box here at the bank, and inside it I found a bunch of diamonds in little Paragon Diamonds bags with markings on them. Seventeen."

"Good grief. Greg didn't tell me. What do the bags say on them? The ones I get have the grades on the outside."

"Most of them say three carats or so and VVS 1 or 2. They're white in color."

"Someone smart needs to look at them, but a three carat, white VVS1 goes for thirty grand these days."

"So there's a half million in the box. Weird."

"Why would Greg have them salted away without telling me?"

"I don't know. I need to bring you up to date. Robertson Investments is bankrupt and a Houston firm is going to file it in bankruptcy. More than likely the SEC would be shutting the firm down soon regardless of whether they file or not. I've distanced myself and Greg's estate from the firm best I can, but you and I should be ready for a bunch of claims being made against the estate and even your community property. The bankruptcy trustee might even make a claim to get back any money you and Greg took out of the firm."

"I can count my lucky stars that my business is separate property. Greg bought the ranch with money he made at the firm. What is that?"

"Depends on the pre-nup agreement you have with him. If there's nothing in it, wages and other income, even from separate property, is community property and liable for claims. We can only wait to see what happens. Gonna be difficult to sort this out."

Given the late hour, after enduring the stressful day I decided to leave early even though it was only four. As I drove home, I noticed another strange vehicle, this time parked on the side of the road at the turnoff from 32. A sedan. Given that I'd found more than a half million in diamonds today, I got paranoid and wrote down the plate number of the sedan. Florida plates.

Carla was happy that I'd gotten out of the Robertson Investments problems, or rather bankruptcy. She was shocked by my treasure find at the bank. I didn't want to dampen Carla's upbeat demeanor, but I needed to confirm that I wasn't being paranoid seeing the vehicles parked by the side of the road. I told her both about the pickup a week ago and the sedan today.

"I don't think it's anything, John. Lots of people do park by the side of the road these days, for cell phone conversations, to figure out where they are, and I suppose to get away and into another environment." I felt better.

Big puffy clouds today. Temperature in the mid-70s, so I took Carla and a bottle of Becker chardonnay out to the gazebo to have a nice, relaxed Friday afternoon. The pipeline dominated our discussions, but we also ran through a catalog of our wild animals. A neighbor had spied a mountain lion recently. The most vicious thing we had here was a raccoon who kept trashing our bird feeders. We kept returning to the pipeline. A massive, multi-billion dollar undertaking. Goliath was intent on bullying its way through Blanco county.

# 11.

As I left for my office in the courthouse Monday morning, I saw a blue Buick SUV across the road on 32 from the turnoff to our place. My paranoia returned, but the way I was going, I couldn't get a good view of the license plate other than to see it wasn't a standard Texas plate.

My office in the courthouse is not magnificent. It's in the southwest corner of the first floor and used to be the county clerk's office before the State moved the county seat to Johnson city. It's the only large office on that floor, five or six hundred square feet, room enough for me to spread out, with a small area for a reception space. The best part is a small nook where county records were kept a century ago that allowed me to have a tiny refrigerator and microwave plus space for soft drinks and even a bit of wine and beer.

When I went into the office, I could tell that someone other than cleaning people had been there. Nothing upset, but papers had been moved. I went through everything. Greg's laptop was missing! The break-in made me fearful and angry at the same time. If you haven't had that happen to you, feel blessed. Even an innocent break-in with nothing disturbed or taken makes you feel insecure, that anything could happen next. Not a professional behind this; he wouldn't have left evidence of his visit. Thankfully, Rob still had the duplicate laptop.

I called Stonewater. "Oliver, you may think I'm paranoid when I tell you this." I told him about the break-in, the missing laptop, and my diamond find and their worth. "I don't know who raided my office, but in the past few days, I've noticed three different vehicles sitting by the road that leads to our house. Unusual. I wrote down the plate number of the one I saw last week, but I couldn't see the plates on the others. My wife thinks there's nothing to it, but I wondered. If the diamonds belong to somebody other than Robertson, I'd think I'd already know, but I can't figure out why Greg would buy and hide such a large cache of diamonds and not tell Sara. I know you're going to be upset that the laptop went missing, but I had the entire laptop copied onto another laptop by our local computer guru here. The guy doing the forensic audit has that computer, so no information is missing."

"As to Robertson's laptop, we too duplicated it before we gave it to you. Never can tell what could happen, like you getting into a wreck that could have damaged the laptop. So don't worry. The stakeouts of your house are another matter. We've got our ways here at the Bureau to find out who's behind vehicle ownership. Give me a day or two and I'll see what's up. You say it was a Florida plate? Give me the number." I did that, and after the call secretly hoped that it would be matched with a lost tourist.

● ● ●

I was relieved when PK called Monday afternoon. I needed a break from the Robertson estate.

"Hey, John. Got every one of my neighbors signed up to flip the sixty foot workspace to the south. It'll save a bunch of trees for me and for my neighbors. My problem is that although I got that done over a week ago, it's been radio silence from Goliath. I need them to confirm that they'll re-engineer the path. Don't have a thing from them. They sure aren't the masters of communication. I don't think they're bad guys tooling me around on purpose, but they're the hardest guys I've ever had to communicate with and get a straight story."

"The whole community dislikes them, judging by the people I talk to and I get from the newspapers," I said. "No one likes a pipeline on their property or in their community, but these guys have made things worse for themselves. I'll call the lawyer on the other side and tell him that unless we get to communicate right away, we'll go back to square one in the litigation, claiming that their route is 'arbitrary and capricious,' the only basis the statute gives us to fight them with."

"And don't forget that they have to sign the papers and pay me the money they promised."

"I'd never let that happen," I said laughing.

"Go get 'em!"

"Thanks. I will."

• • •

Our place— I hesitate to call it a ranch since it's only a hundred acres— is off Cambridge road a quarter of a mile from Ranch

Road 32. Nice and remote. No one drives down our dirt road off Cambridge Road except for three other families who have similar adjoining tracts. That was why I was alarmed when Carla called around 4:30.

"Maybe I was too cavalier when I dismissed your worries about cars on the side of the road. You know, the school bus lets Karen, Kevin and Everett off at Cambridge Road, and unless the weather's bad, they walk the rest of the way home. When they came in, they reported that there was a big, black car parked on Cambridge Road near where they were left off. Since the weather's nice, the driver had his windows down and waved at the kids. Didn't say anything. The kids said he looked big and didn't smile. I quizzed them and they said he was clean shaven, not a hair on his head. I don't know anyone like that around here."

"I'm ahead of you on this. I called Stonewater this morning and asked him to see if he could find out who owned one of the cars I saw the other day. He's working on it. I'll come home right now, and if I can see him, I'll get the license plate of the car he's in.

"Be careful, John. I don't like this. And lock our gate when you come in."

"10-4, as the cops say."

I quickly gathered up the work I was doing for a lawsuit, put the document I was composing on a thumb drive and headed home. There was no one at 32 or on Cambridge Road, or for that matter, on our dirt road. Whoever it was must have figured that the kids would report the strange vehicle.

• • •

Time to tally up Greg's estate. I got Rose to track down where the money to buy the ranch came from, and indeed, it was from his earnings at the firm, which would make it community property, meaning that Sara's half couldn't be reached if Greg's misdoings made the estate liable. I got a copy of Greg and Sara's pre-nup, and the agreement did not provide that the income each had would remain separate, as is now allowed. The problem with that for me was that I had to delve into Sara's accounts, since half of her income from the jewelry business was Greg's. Then I had Rose send me a copy of their last tax return, which offered a trove of information. Took a while. The return was a good two inches thick, and Rose must have cursed me as she copied it. The only surprise was the ranch's income, or rather loss. I knew that Greg ran cattle on his large spread, possibly several hundred, and paid not only Gary's salary but part time workers during parts of the year. Operating the ranch, including Gary's salary, ran well over two hundred grand. Cattle and hay sales only brought in about fifty.

I'd also asked Rose where Greg would keep receipts of any major purchases, wondering whether he kept track somewhere of his diamond purchases. She laughed and said, "That would be the bottom left drawer of Greg's desk. I never looked into it and didn't want to since it is so disorganized. I'll pack it up and send it to you."

I took Rose through the process of what would happen to Robertson Investments, emphasizing that whoever took charge of the firm would need her help, and added that the estate also needed her help. I said she could be assured of a job while every-thing was sorted out, at least a year. She had so much institutional knowledge regarding Robertson and the firm that no one could afford to lose her, but of course I didn't tell her that.

"I've never had anything like this happen to me. I'm an executive secretary, and jobs for people with my skills are hard to find right now. I'll be here, but if ever I plan to leave I'll give you plenty of notice."

"Thanks. I appreciate your sending me the information."

The next day Stonewater called. "John, I've checked out the vehicle, and it's a bit of a dead end. The plate belongs to Hertz and was a rental car. Had to lean a bit on them to spend the time tracking the renter down, but they came up with a company called Security Consultants. They paid with a cash credit card. The address for that company is a New York city drop box, you know, the kind of post office box available at copy centers. A dead end from there, but I've asked Hertz to look into their data for the ID of the driver. Same with the copy center. They should have some information, but for both companies it'll take a few days to dig up old records. Suspicious. What did you say the guy looked like?"

"Big guy, according to my kids. Totally bald head and clean-shaven. Mean looking, older."

"Not much to go on. If you see him again, try to get closer to him for a better description."

"Will do." After I hung up, I googled "Security Consultants" and got a bunch of hits. Too many. Another dead end.

Thankfully Carla had worked at home for the past several weeks compiling three reports on bank audits of small rural banks she'd done. Routine, but the reports called for describing every procedure that go on at a bank. I couldn't do that kind of thing. Not into detail. Carla was so absorbed in the task that each afternoon she had me stop at Loew's, the local grocery store, for supplies. Kevin, now a teenager, has a humongous appetite, and so do the other two, so I usually ended up with two or three full grocery bags.

As I rolled onto Cambridge Road, near our dirt road, I saw a dark GMC Suburban parked, windows up. At first I thought that Tom Maynor, Blanco's police chief, had sent a patrol car to watch our place. Remembering what Stonewater had said, I decided to stop and say hello. My heart was pounding, though, and I was worried what the driver of the car might do. I rolled my window down and pulled up to the car, driver window to driver window.

"Hello," I said as the occupant rolled his window down. Same guy the kids had reported. He looked like a weight lifter and had a droopy right eyelid. Then I saw a small lateral scar across that area of his right eye, more than three inches. Must have been in a knife fight. Like many others in the hill country, he was chewing tobacco, judging by the wad under his lower lip.

The man grunted a hello, but he had a wide smile. "I'm Michael Smith. You live here?" Smith leaned over, causing me a little anxiety that he might be pulling a weapon, but he was only spitting tobacco into a can.

"Yes, down that dirt road. I'm John Mariner. I've seen cars parked around here recently. What's up?"

"Doing a survey of the roads and traffic for a company. I think a pipeline company." He had a bit of an accent. Georgia? Atlanta? Not from here.

"Oh. Strange. They're putting a big pipeline in two miles west of here."

"I don't know. Simply doing what they asked me to do."

"Let me know if you need anything. Will you be doing this for a while?"

"The plan is less than a week more."

"Okay. See ya." I turned into my dirt road, happy that the conversation was over. I called Stonewater from the car and left a voice mail, giving him the description, name and story. I felt sure that the name he gave me was bogus. I wrote the plate number down but didn't pass that along because of the last dead end.

# 12.

I had to go to my office the next morning, which I did warily. Locked the gate to our place as I left. I had to prepare and electronically file a motion to dismiss in a lawsuit that had plagued me for two years. Two adjoining neighbors in a nice subdivision in Blanco had disagreed on where the boundary line was between their two lots. Both got their lots surveyed, and even the surveys differed. Property lines in Blanco are often way off, notwithstanding that a plat had been filed in 1910 showing the city's lots and streets. I'd talked to surveyors about the problem, and each one gave me reasons why their survey was correct and the others wrong. "You know, the earth is round and we're asked to make a flat survey, so surveys are always off a bit" was the most common excuse. The other was that different surveyors started at different points to get to the property being surveyed.

The lawyer opposite me in the lawsuit and I conspired to avoid lengthy and costly litigation between the parties, since we knew that no one could figure out where the real boundary was. The two couples, the other lawyer and I met with a mediator, who helpfully and privately told each of the parties how indeterminate the property line was and how long and costly it would be to have a jury trial, one where the jury would have to flip a coin to decide who was right. That motivated the parties to agree on a boundary line between the two conflicting lines on the two surveys. They agreed to have the two surveyors produce one survey with the new line shown and file it in the deed records. My only task was to get rid of the lawsuit, which I gladly did. Truth is often relative.

Stonewater called. "Jackpot, John. We talked to the rental agency. Hertz. Of course they were reluctant to tell us anything, but when we threatened them with a subpoena and court appearance, they told us what we needed. For the rental they'd recorded the driver's license information. Your friend is Bart Hundley. He lives in Atlanta and runs a business called American Security Specialists, but of course he uses different company names from time to time. Interesting character. I'm surprised he's in your neighborhood. He's nicknamed "Smokey". Perhaps he chain smokes. We have a big file on him. Previously spent twenty years in the Army. Special Forces. Two tours in Afghanistan and one in Iraq and Syria. His problem is he'll take money from anyone. Got in trouble in Cincinnati for planting drugs in a rich lady's car. He wouldn't talk even though we knew that his boss was the woman's ex-husband. Spent twelve months in the hoosegow for that one, breaking and entering and filing a false report with the police—an 'anonymous' call reporting the drugs. On the other hand, he was commended a year ago for rescuing two young children from their mother who was hiding in Mexico, but severely addicted and with mental problems. His client was a techie guy near you, in Austin— the father, to whom the court had given custody of the children. We think Hundley has good connections inside the military and with members of the underworld, particularly the New York mafia."

"What in the world is he doing around Blanco?"

"No telling, but it has to relate either to the Robertson murder or to Goliath's pipeline. Do you have any other rich clients with troubles? Have you irritated the pipeline people?"

"I've got plenty of clients with troubles, but none of them are rich. And while I've been fighting with the pipeline, the relationship's been civil. Must be the Robertson affair. Plenty of pissed off people there."

Stonewater laughed. "If I were you, I'd contact your local county sheriff and the police chief in Blanco and let them know. Hundley needs to know they're watching him."

"But what do they want from me? I'm only the poor lawyer here."

"I always tell my agents that they have to focus on what they don't know. You don't know what motivates the people watching you. Could be benign or threatening. No reason not to be on guard. And tell the family."

That made me shiver. Stonewater continued. "Another thing. We subpoenaed Sara's cell records, and she talked to someone at the Paragon Diamonds number at length and frequently. May simply be business talk, but the flow of the calls makes us suspicous. Several days prior to Robertson's trip to the ranch, she talked for twenty minutes several times a day to someone there. Then totally quiet. Then the day of the crash, once she must have found out that the crash had occurred, she called again, several times into the evening. Then again twenty minute calls several times a day for two days, then short calls after that twice a week until now. Keep this confidential for now since what we see may be normal business chitchat."

That stymied me, given my impression that Sara was a bit naïve and was only buying diamonds off the shelf, as it were, from Paragon. I had to push ahead in any event. To get my mind off the surveillance by Hundley, I dove into totting up Greg's assets. Half the ranch was worth three million, but how to use that to pay off creditors, especially the Bank of America loan, puzzled me. I'd have to get Sara to sell the ranch. She wasn't really attached to it. Maybe selling it right away wouldn't be a problem, but there are few multi-millionaires wandering around with a checkbook big enough to cover a six million dollar ranch purchase. His and Sara's home in Houston was exempt but had to be valued. River Oaks. Another several million, but I'd never seen it. I'd have to rely on Rose's list for the rest of his assets. Rose, Sara and I would have to work together to get values, like his cars, personal items, jewelry and odd possessions like weapons. I'd get someone local to value the ranch vehicles and equipment. Some people have too much stuff. That would take time.

And then there was the diamond treasure. I got the name of a diamond appraiser in Austin. I didn't think it'd be smart to leave the diamonds with anyone, so I planned to take documents to revise while the appraiser did his work.

Carla called in a state of alarm. "John, someone broke into our home! While the kids were in school, I went to San Marcos to shop, and I was gone three hours. When I got home a few minutes ago, the door was unlocked. I could tell someone had been in the house, and for a while I worried about going in, thinking whoever it was might still be in there. I got up the courage to go in, and looked around. Nothing was taken and the house was still in order, but I could tell someone had rifled through our bedroom drawers and your office drawers, including the file cabinet and your desk. I'm sure I locked the door, as I always do, and I'm also sure I closed the gate to the house. Of course, without a lock, the gate's easy to open, but with our Andersen doors, with their double action, it's not easy to get in."

"Were the windows locked?"

"Hmmm. I don't know. Since it's early spring, I might have pulled windows down without locking them. I'll check."

"I need to report it to Bob Hauffler, our long-time county sheriff. Bob'll send a deputy out to take the report. Stonewater told me to call him anyway about the break-in at my office and the missing laptop. Sounds like the same sloppy thief who hit my office, probably Hundley." I brought Carla up to date on Hundley and his surveillance program. That would explain why he'd been lurking around, waiting to make sure that the house was unoccupied when he went in. What was he looking for?

"Bob, how are you?" I said when I called our long-time sheriff. I got a litany of his troubles. "Sorry, Bob, I meant that rhetorically." He laughed.

"What can I do for you?" I told him about the mysterious cars and the break-in, including my conversations with the FBI.

"You sure do know how to get yourself in trouble. That Hundley guy sounds dangerous. We'll start looking for him. In the meantime, I'll send a deputy out to your house to take the report from Carla. Let me see who's available.

"The damned pipeline is straining my resources. A huge project. I can't think of anyone local who is supportive of the pipeline coming in. They've insisted on my making patrols along the areas they've marked for the pipeline since they have survey stakes and directional signs at intersections. Lots of vocal opponents around here, and Goliath thinks that a number of them are ready to tear down their signs to slow down their efforts until March 15."

"Why is that date important?"

"Believe it or not, new construction, that is, clearing the pipeline path, has to stop then. Golden-cheeked warbler nesting season. It's an endangered species, and the feds have ordered them to leave the area alone till mid-July."

I had to laugh. Hundreds of humans opposing the pipeline, but only a small bird could stop their progress.

"It's not funny to Goliath. They're calling the disruption sabotage. To me, if anything happens, the protestors should only be charged with malicious mischief or trespassing. A misdemeanor, not a felony. But the pipeline reps reminded me that in 2019, the legislature made it a third-degree felony to even protest pipeline construction if it impedes progress. I'd hate to put any local residents, even rambunctious ones, in jail for protesting like that."

"Glad I'm not in your shoes."

"Bad and good though. A number of locals are getting rich off this. Think of the strain on our restaurants and stores when hundreds of workers come into the county. The police in Blanco and Johnson city are working off-duty long hours and getting paid well to sit there and make sure no one is pulling up stakes. It's gonna be crazy around here for a year or so."

# 13.

I needed a break so arranged to go to Gemstone Appraisers, LLC, in Austin the next day, waiting for the rush hour and school traffic to clear. I first went to the bank and picked up the stones, carrying the diamonds in a standard legal briefcase in case someone was watching me. Hal had coached me how to look out for someone tailing me, but the way sophisticated people tail people these days made me wonder whether I'd be able to tell if someone was following me. To make sure, when I got to Dripping Springs, I circled around, going through the street next to the HEB grocery store, down to the YMCA, then right back to the route 12 road and back to 290. No one behind me that I could tell. The appraisal company was off Route 1, Mopac as it's known, three miles north of 290. Again, I turned off at Rudy's Barbeque and circled through their parking lot to see whether anyone was behind me. Since it was only eleven, few people were at the restaurant, and I couldn't see anyone following me. I was tempted to go in and get a little barbeque but resisted the temptation.

Austin's grown so much that traffic everywhere is bad. I had to wait several minutes before I could break into the traffic, with cars going sixty, well over the speed limit. Still no one in sight.

The diamond appraisal office was in a three-story office building. Spartan but clean and brightly lit. I wasn't sure that many people actually came to their office. Any wealthy owner of diamonds needing an appraisal could simply ask the appraiser to come to their home or business. A fortyish, well-groomed man came into the small reception area. "Hi, I'm Chad. I talked to you on the phone. Thanks for your business. I know you're worried about the stones, so if you want, you can come back into my office where I have my evaluation equipment and you can watch me do my thing."

"Great. I'll do that." We went into his room, and an array of instruments stood along a workbench running the length of his fifteen-foot wall. Mostly microscope-looking things. A desk sat opposite the equipment area, and Chad motioned for me to use the desk.

He worked over the stones for two hours, making notes on each stone as he went. He didn't say much the whole time, only occasionally making a small grunt or breathing out heavily as he finished one or another stone.

"You've got an amazing collection here. These are the best and biggest diamonds I've seen in a while. Diamond prices have gone up over the past year, and I want to confirm the prices with a few comparisons, but my initial reaction is that you've got three quarters of a million dollars in stones here. Do you know anything about their provenance?"

"Their what?"

"Their provenance, where they came from. I see that the stones are in packages from a company called Paragon Diamonds."

"Yes, they're in the diamond district in New York city. I have no idea where Paragon got them, but I presume the owner bought them there and was holding them for investment."

"Diamonds have a troubled history as an investment. Gold's better. Diamond prices swing too much depending on the state of the world."

"To tell you the truth, as you know, the diamonds are owned by a guy named Greg Robertson, and the FBI is convinced that he was murdered. They also suspect that the diamonds are blood diamonds because of Paragon's history."

"If the country of origin of the diamonds hasn't been certified by the Kimberley Process, valuing these is a crap shoot. Most reputable houses won't buy non-certified diamonds. They have value though. Maybe half or a third. No place much to sell them. Do you have any certifications?"

"No. I found these diamonds in a safety deposit box. I'll call Sal Minardi at Paragon Diamonds and find out."

I left Austin as traffic was getting heavy, but Rudy's Barbeque beckoned me. I stopped there to pig out on brisket, and bought a pint of their good creamed corn to take home for Carla. The smell of the creamed corn and left-over brisket filled my pickup as I drove home, keeping me from fretting over what I should do with the diamonds. People at Rudy's must have thought I was weird carrying a briefcase through the order line, but I couldn't let the diamonds out of my sight. I stopped at the bank and put the stones back into the safety deposit. Too late to call New York.

I'd do that first thing tomorrow. No one following and no one lurking at the gate.

When I got home, the weather being bad, to keep from talking in front of the kids, Carla and I went into my home office so that I could bring her up to date and give her comfort that whoever broke into our house had found nothing and wouldn't be visiting us again. After I told her about Smokey Hundley, she got concerned all over again, mainly for our physical safety and that of the kids.

"I don't think there's any danger, really. Whoever broke in was looking for something. Probably the diamonds. Or the laptop," I said, remembering the office break-in.

"If Greg didn't commit suicide, he was murdered. That's more probable, and if someone is willing to kill Greg, he wouldn't hesitate to kill others. I hate it when you get involved like this with clients. I worry about you."

● ● ●

Bob Hauffler called. "What the hell is going on around PK's place?"

"I have no idea what you're talking about."

"Goliath is calling every police and sheriff's department in the area. They say that people up and down the pipeline route are out there protesting and may become violent. They want our officers to do off-duty protection for their pipeline project, 24-7."

"Wow. Are they worried that the protestors will pull up the survey stakes and signage?"

"More serious than that. They think someone might disable their equipment, you know, the digging equipment and the Bobcats and other big equipment they use to tear out trees and bushes and handle the pipe as it's being welded. Goliath studied protests at other pipelines, and protestors did make life miserable for those involved in constructing the pipeline. Worse yet, they sneak into storage yards and take drills to the pipeline segments that are stored. They drill a hole little more than half way in. When the pipeline is installed and pressure-tested, the line blows up. Scares everyone within miles and raises the protest level. So every pipe segment has to be X-rayed inch by inch before it's put in the ground."

"Sounds pretty sophisticated. Like Robertson's crash."

"Yeah. You'd be surprised how much money those protestors have behind them. Three lawsuits still around trying to stop the pipeline. PK is one of the contributors, and he's rich and knowledgeable because he ran an office-building construction company. I hope he's fighting them with words and nothing else. And this Hundley guy being in the area bothers me. He has the sophistication and knowledge to pull bad things off. Did he know that you represent the city and PK in the pipeline lawsuits?"

"I have no idea, unless PK contacted him or someone at the city told him. My name's been in the paper with stories reporting on both pipeline suits. That could be the way he knows."

"Okay, but check with PK. Don't want him involved in any mischief."

"Will do. By the way does the city or your department get anything out of their using your officers for security?"

"Sure. They need to use patrol cars, so we basically rent out our older ones to them so that the off-duty officers can man the vehicles and watch the goings on. We're getting two thousand a month from that. We can use the money to upgrade our vehicles to new technology. With that and the cut we get from the cash we get from seizing money from drug dealers when we arrest them, we're the most up to date police department in central Texas."

I had to laugh. "I'll call PK and make sure he's standing down."

"They'll be around the rest of the year. I'm looking forward to their moving east of the county."

"So am I, but I'm sure Hays county isn't looking forward to their arrival."

# 14.

The next few days were tranquil. I knew it wouldn't last. The city Council meeting that Tuesday turned out to be more tumultuous than usual. Those protesting the new sewer plant mingled with the ones protesting the pipeline. The city suffers from growing pains. Fortunately, the protests were vocal; none of them looked particularly prone to violence. More than half were over 65.

If I were mayor I'd turn the regular agenda upside down. At the beginning of every meeting, after the Pledge of Allegiance, the public is invited to make a statement, and sometimes the statements, notwithstanding the three minute time limit, ramble on. If I'd been in charge of the agenda, I would have put the public statements last on the agenda. This night there were seventeen citizens asking to talk, and the mayor, Jim Roberts, presided with his usual affable demeanor. Twelve complained about the sewer plant and its compliance with environmental rules and the high cost of the new sewer plant and water plant. The others protested against the pipeline going through town, afraid of the risk of explosion and the environmental damage. Jim listened taciturnly, smiling often as speakers attacked him and the city. Finally, after over an hour of this, Jim returned to the agenda. The mayor, in charge of what was on the agenda, always put "Remarks by the Mayor" at the top of the agenda, right after the public statement period.

Jim began with a smile. "I can tell y'all that the city has good news. First and foremost you need to know that the sewer and the water plants have been designed by the highest quality engineering firms specializing in those things. They're familiar with the rules. On top of that, we have the Texas Commission on Environmental Quality, the TCEQ, thoroughly involved in the process. As you know, they've been on our backs for years because of our sixty-year-old sewer plant that's out of compliance.

"Second, for those of you who are concerned about our finances, I'd like to announce that the city has settled with Goliath. At the end of the day, we can't stop them from coming through our city. We can't make them move the line. They've got all the cards. After long discussions, Goliath agreed to pay us one million dollars in exchange for our granting them an easement under city properties and roads. They also agreed to repair any roads damaged by their equipment. We'll use the million to reduce the five million dollar cost of our new sewer and water plants. This means we have a satisfactory deal that'll assure the city of its financial soundness and gives Goliath what they are legally entitled to anyway. We'll put the million in the bank and, with the million five we already have, that fund will assure us that we have the money to make the quarterly payments on the bonds we have to finance the plants without having to raise rates by more than cost of living increases."

For a moment the crowd was silent. And then someone started clapping, followed by the entire room joining in. Half the crowd left, half of them smiling and the other half chagrined. I figured those leaving were equally split between the sewer and water plant group and the pipeline group, the latter still holding out hope that somehow the pipeline wouldn't come through our city and county. I sat back, ready to go through the remaining items, every one of them mundane and uncontroversial. After two and a half hours, I was ready to go home and have a late dinner. The kids would be getting ready for bed.

Around noon the next day, Tom Maynor, the city's police chief, called. "John, I thought you'd want to know. Officer Kemmerer was on patrol this morning and saw a guy lurking around the entrance to the Texas Regional Bank, sitting on the bench outside. Fred approached him to find out what he was doing, since he stands out. Big and muscular, wearing a camouflage shirt and pants, odd since it's not hunting season. He did identify himself. It was Smokey Hundley, the guy you said Bob Hauffler's deputies have been on the lookout for. When Fred asked him if he was in town to hunt feral hogs or axis deer, Hundley clammed up and told Fred it was none of his business, saying 'I've got nothing further to say to you.' Fred said okay and left, but recommended that we keep a lookout for him. He gave the bank people a heads up that Hundley was hanging around the bank in case he had an agenda there. Odd."

"Sure is." I told Tom how I'd found the diamond treasure at the bank and filled him in on the break-in at my office.

"We'll keep an eye on him. No telling what he's doing around here. He could even be working for Goliath or for Goliath's opponents. He'd know how to sabotage the pipeline given his background."

• • •

I had to unlock the heritage of the diamond treasure. I called Sal Minardi but got his voice mail twice, announcing who I was and what I wanted. The third time he answered. I could tell he was apprehensive.

"Hi, Sal. I presume that you were told Greg Robertson died."

"Yes, Sara told me. I think I know what you're calling for. The diamonds Greg had."

"That's one thing. Yes. What's the story?"

"Not much to tell. I never thought that he'd do this to me. The son of a bitch. Greg bought the diamonds when he was in town for meetings. Two or three at a time over a year or so. I looked and the checks he gave me were always on an account styled 'Gregory Robertson—Separate Account'. He always asked for invest-ment grade diamonds with three to four carats. Said they were for investment, not Sara. Pledged me to confidentiality, but that's over since he's died. My problem is that he bought four from me the month before he died, and he never paid for the stones. A hundred-fifty grand he still owes Paragon. On top of that, I got Paragon to invest seventeen million with his firm, and I'm getting stonewalled by his people. I need to know what my company's account is worth and how I get my money back. Seventeen million one is big money for Paragon and me."

"I'm only the executor of his estate and I don't run Robertson Investments. Please email me a copy of the statement or whatever showing what his estate owes you, as well as copies of any checks and the account number if you can find it. Need it for the probate proceeding. While you're at it, send me any information you have on your investment account at the firm and I'll pass it along and try to find out where you stand. Now for the more difficult question.

Need to ask it for valuing the diamonds. Were they certified by the Kimberley Process or the Canadians?"

"You're a quick study. I don't know whether they were certified by our Belgian supplier or not. Since they were not going to one of the big houses, I didn't ask. The prices were cut rate for their quality, and I passed on the savings to Greg. Judging by the price, I presume not. Listen, John, don't push too hard on this. The people here and the ones we deal with are not nice people. I hate to think what will happen to me if I don't get Paragon's money back."

"Don't you own Paragon?"

"Not really. I've got a profit-sharing deal with the owners. That's all I can tell you."

"Let's take this one step further. Let me gather the facts to understand where Paragon stands in relation to others involved with Robertson Investments. I'll check with you if I need anything more." With that I said my good-byes and hung up. I hated to think about the reverberations to come when Sal finds out that Robertson Investments filed for bankruptcy. That would happen in the next day or two. I needed to look up the real account balance for Paragon.

• • •

Tom Maynor called the next day. "John, I've got a legal problem. Those Goliath people are up in arms. As you know, half of my officers have been working off duty as security officers for Goliath, using our older patrol vehicles. Last night, someone went into PK's property. We don't know when, but our officer left the area around one. When Goliath's contractors arrived for work at eight, they found that the bobcat and the excavator, you know, the thing with a sort of claw, had been vandalized. Distributor caps gone, ignition wires cut, bolts loosened here and there, then doused with diesel and set on fire. Goliath is in an uproar since it'll take a week or ten days to replace the equipment. The damage, they say, will run into the thousands. By the time they haul off the damaged equipment and replace everything, they'll have to stop clearing until mid-July since it's the yellow-cheeked warbler mating season. A costly problem for them, but of course they and Goliath are blaming us and threatening to sue the city. That's bullshit. They told us to monitor all day except between one and six am. My officers can't go into private property without permission, so they have to park on the shoulders of public roads. No one saw anything. Are we going to be sued?"

"Settle down, Tom. Is there a written contract or anything like that between the city and Goliath?"

"Nope. All verbal."

"They can't sue the city because of the verbal rental of police vehicles. Vehicles can't commit sins. And Goliath knew that the officers were off duty and paid them directly as part time contractors. Unless they can show that the officers involved were negligent, say ignored suspicious circumstances, they aren't liable either. Seems to me they're the ones responsible since they didn't call for coverage between one and six."

Silence on the other end. Then Tom spoke up. "That makes sense. I hate to see the city threatened like that. I don't like those guys, even though they're throwing money around the city and county like drunken sailors."

"I hear you. People say things they shouldn't when they're upset. I'm sure this has thrown a real wrench in their plans. They're already behind schedule six months, and this isn't helping. I'll let you know if I hear anything."

"I'll talk to the mayor," I offered.

"You don't think that Hundley dude was behind this, do you?"

"Don't know. By what you've told me, only someone familiar with mechanical equipment could have done the vandalizing. Meanwhile I'll call PK and make sure he's not involved in this."

"Let me know if you learn anything."

I called PK. He laughed when he answered. "I bet I know why you're calling. No, I didn't have a thing to do with what's going on. In fact, I'm mad at whoever did it. I've got all sorts of people crawling over the property—cops, Goliath executives in fancy duds, repairmen, and gawkers. My cattle have run over to the other side of that pasture. Couldn't happen to a nicer bunch of bullies. Payback. I have no idea who could have done it. I suppose they came into the property through the Goliath access gates and paths. If I had a mind to do that, I'd have done it on someone else's place, not my own. Besides, I don't know the difference between a distributor cap and a spark plug."

It was my turn to laugh. "Good to hear that, PK. I didn't think you were involved, and I hope those yokels get off your property quickly. Sorry that happened to you."

"I was looking forward to their leaving. They've pulled the trees down and cleared the entire easement area. Sad to see. My wife won't go see the devastation right now. Now they'll be here for a while since they'll have to do some of the repairs to the big exca- vator on site. It's not running, and it's too big to try to haul away if it's not working. Maybe my cows will get curious and eat up the wires on their equipment."

"Let's stay clear of them for now. Goliath has their hands full, and contractors always find someone to blame other than themselves."

"Amen. Take it easy."

# 15.

Rose called. "John, the firm filed for bankruptcy this morning. Paul told me it was called a liquidating 11. What does that mean?"

"That means that they're going to liquidate the firm, but instead of what's called a straight bankruptcy, a Chapter 7, they're going to do it through the reorganization Chapter 11. That way the firm, rather than a bankruptcy trustee, will be in charge of the liquidation. The main task will be to find another firm to take over the customer accounts as a starting point."

"Will I have a job?"

"For sure. You know where everything is, so they'll be depending on you to help out. These things go on forever, so I think you're safe for at least a year. We'll need your help with the estate too."

"Good. I've been helping Rob sort out the two sets of books Greg was keeping. I'm afraid most customer accounts are half of what each investor put in at the beginning. The investors will be mad. Greg's own accounts are down to a tenth of his original investment. Looks as if he tried speculating to catch back up. That didn't work."

"Make sure what you're doing is clear and accurate, since the records will be filed in the bankruptcy court."

"Yes, that's what Rob told me. Paul wants him to continue working for us, but Rob said he needed to be paid in advance. Paul told him the court needed to approve that, but Rob said he could be paid and then have the court confirm the payment. What a different world this is from what I was doing!"

"Mine too." After we hung up, I needed advice to help me figure out what the truth was. I called Hal and met with him over coffee at the Blanco Bowling Alley and Club. The bowling alley is a local and national institution. One of three nine-pin bowling alleys left in the State of Texas. The restaurant in the front of the building offers a fare straight out of the 1940's—I don't think they'd ever changed the menu. I opted for a slice of their lemon meringue pie, a giant slice with a three-inch meringue topping. My lunch.

I brought Hal up to date on what I knew about the plane crash, Paragon and the diamond treasure, Greg's troubles, and Sara's relationship with Greg and with Paragon. "Hal, so many clues have popped up that I'm having trouble sorting out where this is going. I can't finish the estate until I know the explanation for Greg's death. Several things point to his being done in by people he'd screwed, like Paragon Diamonds. He owed them a large amount of money and stonewalled them. They're not nice people. Same story with two mysterious LLCs we can't identify. Each one invested ten million. No trace of them although there are email inquiries from SwissBank asking for information and current account values. Doesn't look like Greg answered any of those emails.

"On the other hand, looking into Greg's mindset, suicide's a possibility. He must've known he was running out of alternatives.

His customers didn't know that they'd lost half the funds they'd given him. His own wealth had dwindled down to close to nothing by his making speculative trades to get back to square one. The pressure was on him, and I'm sure that contributed to his relationship with Sara going to pieces. For him the only solution might have been to stage an accident so that the insurance policy could pay off for his brothers and Sara. Insurance proceeds are exempt from creditors. What do you think's the case?"

"We're not done here yet. We need more facts, especially Paragon and the Sal guy. As you've said, since he owed that gang a large amount, they'd be unlikely to kill him, which would frustrate any hopes of getting their money back. On the other hand, if they somehow knew that their money was lost, their attitude could have changed. When I say that, I assume that Paragon's a criminal enterprise. I should call the New York office and let them know what you've told me. Don't know who's behind that company, but I'm sure they're not legit. Could be the Mafia or more likely a Mexican cartel using Paragon to launder money. That said, I'd go for the suicide alternative, and you should expect the insurance company to contest the policy payment. That'll keep your estate open for a long time."

"That's not good. I'm not sure that there'll be enough money to pay the lawyers to defend the lawsuits coming the estate's way—the insurance company, the investors, and the SEC."

"I'd spend my time looking for more information on the LLCs and Paragon. If there's a killer around, he's got to be inside one of those companies."

"What about Sara? Not all of her customers were high class. Look at I4U2 and his rapper buddies. Those calls with Paragon are strange."

"She could be more sophisticated and may know a lot more than she's telling you. Sounds as if her relationship with Paragon was deeper than you think. Money talks. Even though she might not be capable of staging the accident, there's always somebody out there to do whatever a mind can concoct. Even though both Sara and the rapper have plenty of money to get things done, the sophistication of the airplane crashing makes me think a bigger organization is involved."

"But if it's the Mafia or one of the cartels, why wouldn't they just make Greg disappear? Like Jimmy Hoffa."

Hal laughed. "They never did find Hoffa's body, but we know why he was done in. Finding the body's not important. The mob didn't want him returning to run the Teamsters. The reason they might have killed Greg the way they did simply sends a message to others not to cross the bad guys and their money."

"That sends shivers down my back again. I wish I knew how to keep my distance from them."

"That's easy. Take Carla's advice and stay passive. Let the FBI and the SEC sort this out. That'll take time. Look at how long it's taken to sort out Hoffa."

• • •

PK called my cell but from an odd number. He had memorized my number. "I can't believe this! I'm at the county jail in Johnson city and they're arresting me. They claim I'm the one who messed up their equipment on my property."

"Calm down, PK. I'll come up right away, but the municipal judge has to set the bond amount before I can get you out. What are you charged with?"

"Don't know for sure, but a deputy said malicious destruction of property, a felony."

"I'll help out, but you need an experienced criminal defense lawyer if you're charged with a felony. I'll check with Bob Hauffler and the county Attorney, Rebecca Watler, to see why they're doing this."

I knew that PK was a hothead, but he's smart. I doubted that he'd destroy equipment on his own property. I called Bob.

"Bob, what's up with PK?"

"I shouldn't be talking to you about this, but it's serious. More than the vandalism that happened on his property two days ago. Last night, along Chimney Valley Road, a pickup drove up to the site where Goliath has begun pulling off the topsoil, preparing it for the big dig. Whoever was in that pickup then went over to the bulldozer, poured diesel over it and under it and lit it up. The perpetrator who did it didn't realize that one of my deputies was down the road in his car watching the guy. The light from the blaze lit up things enough that he ID'd the pickup as PK— white with a light bar on top. I suppose people use those light bars to see at night when they're hunting in the dark."

"Definitely serious. Did your deputy have a description of the guy?"

"Not much to go on. Temperature was 50, so the guy had a coat on and a western hat. Bandana covering his face. The problem was that when the deputy turned on his service flashlight and pointed it at the guy, a shot rang out from somewhere. Not the individual. The deputy doused the light, got back into the car, and high tailed it out of the area. This dang pipeline is getting dangerous."

"I'll get PK bonded out and then talk to Becky. Unless your deputy has a positive ID of PK or the truck, she'll be hesitant to prosecute. What you say isn't very compelling to me. PK's not the only white pickup in Blanco county with a light bar. PK'll be open with me, and I know he'll deny he did that, but I'll plumb the depths of his story and make sure it was not him."

"We can't take chances, John. I want to send a message to the community that violence against the pipeline won't be tolerated, much as I hate to see it go in. I secretly sympathize with those opposing it."

"Before you do anything, let's get more facts. The arrest could boomerang on the department if you arrested the wrong person, especially if it was my vocal and well-known client who was wronged."

"Yeah, I agree. I'll tell my guys to keep the arrest quiet till we find out more."

# 16.

Except for PK's problems, life in Blanco returned to normal, it seemed. No sign of Smokey Hundley for several weeks, no one lurking around our home or my office and no protests alarming the community. All thanks to the golden-cheeked warbler. Since Goliath had to stall its construction schedule until July 15, it concentrated on the parts of the line they'd cleared before March 15. Hauffler said that they'd be boring under the various roads and river crossings they needed to go under to avoid changing the landscape too much or exposing the pipe, either of which would have gotten the environmentalists going. Word was that they'd bore twenty feet under each crossing to avoid pipe exposure for the next century.

I thought, or rather observed, that the process of identifying the landowners along the pipeline route, getting the easements, clearing the path and then digging the pipeline was quite disorganized. As Muhammed Ali said, "Everyone's got a plan until the first punch hits home." Weather, protesters, and difficult terrain put Goliath a good nine months or more behind schedule. Same with every multi-billion dollar project.

Of course PK denied involvement in the incident, but I was troubled by the deputy's description of the pickup. Light bars on vehicles aren't registered, and many pickups have them. A thought came to me: the local voluntary fire departments in the area—four of them—encouraged their volunteers to place light bars on their vehicles, ones with flashing colored lights, to use when they were racing to a fire or accident. That meant that there had to be dozens of pickups with light bars driving around Blanco county. I got an appointment with Becky Watler, the district attorney, and went to her office in Johnson city early that Tuesday, oddly April Fool's Day. I hoped that wasn't a portent of things to come.

"John, I haven't seen you since the pre-election Republican candidate gatherings! I hope you're well."

"Sure am." I figured she didn't need to be bored with my other stresses, the Robertson revelations and the city's issues. "You know what I'm here for. Can we quietly dismiss the case against PK?"

"Hard to do given the arrest. Frankly, I'm planning on sitting on the case for a while, having taken to heart Hauffler's own concerns that the IDs the deputy reported weren't that definitive."

I related my thoughts about the voluntary fire department light bars common in the area, and she let out a deep breath. "I haven't passed this on to a grand jury, and there's no indictment out there, only the arrest. If no other evidence shows up in the next six months, I'll recommend that the charges be dismissed for lack of evidence. Knowing you, I think you'd convince any jury that there was reasonable doubt that your client was the bad guy, even though he may in fact have done it. For now, since the arrest isn't published in the local newspapers, no one will know about it, but you might want to tell PK to cool it for a while."

I had to laugh. "You've got a tough job, Becky, but to make you feel better, I talked to PK extensively, and he's adamant that neither he nor any of his people did the vandalizing or shooting. His main defense is simple—why would I initiate vandalism when my own property was under close scrutiny?"

Becky nodded and waited.

"I understand your position. PK and I will stand down and let this incident age a little. Thanks!"

• • •

Back to my office. I called PK, asking him to stand down from doing anything. Or saying anything about his arrest or Goliath and the pipeline. His visibility as a pipeline opponent made him suspect.

My office comforts me. It's a relaxing place. Normally I park on the south side of the courthouse and come in through that door. Right inside is the back door into my office, right at my desk. Clients come through another door, near the west side courthouse door. I don't have that many clients coming to me, so I leave it locked. As I sat down, ready to work, a loud knock on the door reverberated through my office. Since I didn't expect anyone and didn't want to spend time with someone soliciting me for a contribution, I walked over and asked who it was.

"My name's Bart Hundley and I need to talk to you." Adrenaline rushed through me. Took a few minutes for me to decide whether to let him in. I didn't know whether Dot Krieger, the executive director of the courthouse, had come to work yet or not. If she hadn't arrived, there wouldn't be anyone to yell out to if he had violence in mind. I decided to take a chance and let him in. In person he looked bigger and more muscular that he'd seemed when I talked to him in his car on my road two weeks before. And meaner. He had an open carry pistol on his right hip.

"Hello. Good to see you again. I don't know if you remember me from our introduction outside your road the other day. My real name is Bart Hundley."

"I know your name, Smokey. The authorities have been following you around here."

That knocked him off guard, which I'd intended to do. "They're watching me?"

"Yes, and they gave me a full rundown on your background. What do you want with me?"

Smokey paused, collecting himself. "All right. You should know what I'm here for. My client wants those diamonds Robertson bought back. They're trying to limit their losses, seeing as how his firm filed bankruptcy last week."

I could tell that Smokey was as nervous as I was. Had to think of a way to get rid of him. "No can do, Smokey, even if I wanted to. You see, the assets of Robertson Investments and even of Greg Robertson are locked down on court order. The diamonds are under lock and key, and if they go anywhere, it's jail time for whoever takes them. And I know, given your record, that you don't want to spend any more time lolling around in a jail in Houston. That place is not fit for human habitation. To get them you'll have to get a court order from the bankruptcy court."

That stymied Hundley. Frustrated, he said, "You'd better be telling me the truth. My people are not the forgiving sort. Watch your back. Something might happen to you like it happened to Robertson." With that he turned and walked out the client door.

That shook me. It occurred to me that his threat was a felony all by itself because of the ongoing investigation of Greg's death and the firm's financial troubles. I knew that whoever was paying Hundley had to be a big organization, likely a criminal one. I felt defenseless. I decided to put Hauffler and Maynor on a conference call with Hal and me and report what had been said, including the threats. "Was everything you said about the diamonds the truth?" Hal asked.

"Pretty much so. My sense right now is that Greg's estate will have to file bankruptcy too. Giving up an asset or money right now, immediately before a filing, is called a preference, and the bankruptcy court can set it aside. Doing that could also lead to criminal charges if done intentionally. Sorta half true. But I haven't verified where the money for the diamonds came from. If Greg took it out of the firm and put the money in his separate account, the diamonds would belong to the firm and would be subject to the stay order not to tamper with any assets. I'm not sure Smokey would have appreciated those nuances while I talked him out of doing anything right now."

Hauffler laughed. "Tom, I don't have the funds or people to do this, but John and his family need looking after. Can you spare anyone to watch over John?"

"I've got overtime funds left, and the fiscal year is ending soon, so I can burn up a little of that. I'll do that for the time being."

Hal piped up. "John, could you put those diamonds into a court registry?"

"Good idea. I'd sure like to get rid of them. I'll call the firm's bankruptcy lawyers and make sure they know that the title to the diamonds is up in the air."

We adjourned the call, promising to have a call every few weeks to compare notes. I didn't look forward to telling Carla what the day had brought, but I had to. Hundley and his clients were after me, not my family, but I couldn't take a chance with that.

# 17.

I called Susan Becker, the lawyer handling the Robertson Investments bankruptcy, the next morning while I was sitting in the gazebo by our pond. Spring had arrived. The wildflowers were abundant around our place, except for bluebonnets. I think that bluebonnets need good dirt to thrive, and our place offered only rocky, thin soil. Even where we had inviting places for grass and flowers, the depth of the dirt had to be less than an inch or two.

"Susan, how is the bankruptcy going?"

"Very complicated, but we lawyers love complexities, don't we? Once we met with Rob, Rose and Paul and reviewed the history, we converted Robertson Investments into a straight Chapter 7 liquidation. It'll take several years to sort everything out and get money back from those that got out early so that money can be re-allocated to those who left their money in. Why no one questioned Greg Robertson's actions bewilders me. The markets went up and down, but the accounts he sent to his clients varied only slightly, even when a market dip occurred. Since Robertson himself constructed this house of cards, there'll be multi-million dollar claims against him by the trustee and others. Given the collapse of the accounts at the firm because of his speculating, you can bet the trustee will hammer his estate."

That meant me, the executor. "Who's the trustee in bankruptcy?"

"The judge appointed Bruce Silverton. Thankfully he's sophisticated financially and has a world of experience in bankruptcy law. We've been retained by Bruce to continue representing the firm's bankrupt estate, but our fees will be a fraction of what they would've been in an 11."

"Can you recommend someone who you could work with if I file the estate in bankruptcy?"

"Sure. I'll send two or three names and you can pick. Linda Wilcox is my favorite, but she'll stand up for the estate if there's a conflict between the firm and the estate."

"I'll go with her. Thanks for the update." I called Wilcox, explained the entire mess and the position of Greg's estate. She hesitated momentarily but then agreed to represent Greg's estate if I could muster up a retainer of ten thousand. I took care of that immediately, as I didn't want to go further without a lawyer myself.

Bummer. Ben Reeder needed to know where we were. I called him and brought him up to date on the diamonds, Hundley, and the Robertson Investments bankruptcy. Then he started.

"I hate to pile on bad news, John, but the Alliance Insurance Company yesterday sent me a long letter denying payment on the six million dollar insurance policy. They claim that Greg committed suicide. They've talked to your friend Susan Becker and had an investigator follow up with the SEC and the NTSB. They're taking a risk, since Texas law says non-payment will increase the principal by ten per cent if it's ultimately determined that the policy should have been paid. It's an asset of the estate, but if the policy is paid, the estate will get nothing—the beneficiaries will. It's up to them to decide if they want to fund a complex lawsuit. What do you want me to do now?"

I was at a loss to think of anything. "We have to stay involved in the insurance claim since it will be the estate that will have to defend against the insurance company's denial. Greg took the policy out a bare three months and a day before the crash, so the money that Greg paid for the policy or the entire proceeds could be a bankruptcy preference that would allow the firm's bankruptcy trustees for the estate or for the firm to demand the six million, or at least the premium, which was probably less than five thousand. Thank God you and I will only be spectators for that. For the time being, I'm going to go back to Chad Wiseman at Diamond Appraisers and see whether he can find a buyer for the diamonds so you and I can get an advance on our fees. This drama will go on for a long time, and having gotten in, the courts won't let us out."

"True. I appreciate your looking out after me."

So much for a laconic morning in the gazebo. The mood was tainted, so I went in and got ready for the office. Along the way I told Carla what was going on. Typical reply.

"I know that you're totally immersed in the Robertson thing, but to me this is working out well. Sounds as if the estate needs to file bankruptcy too, and that way, you'll be relieved of the stress in putting things right. The only thing they'll need you for is selling the ranch. And knowing you, you'll want to be at every bankruptcy hearing and the litigation on the insurance policy. As a spectator."

●  ●  ●

At least one irritant in my life resolved itself. The Goliath pipeline controversy rolled over everyone objecting to the installation of the pipeline across the hill country. Counties, cities, landowners, and environmentalists were swept away, given the law allowing a private company to condemn property without any hearing to justify the condemnation other than to set a value for the loss in value of the property. And no compensation for the use of the land during the installation. Those choosing to fight the value Goliath wanted to pay would have to wait literally years before they saw any money. Goliath would have so-called experts testify that after five years the land will have healed. No testimony regarding the trees they proposed to take down. The law needed to be changed, but this being an energy-producing state, reform was not in the wind. Not fair. At least if PK kept quiet for a while, the charges against him would go away.

Back to my own little world. That is, my pocketbook. The more I heard from Houston and the FBI and SEC, the more worried I was that Greg's estate would have to file Chapter 7 bankruptcy too. I needed to get Ben's and my fees paid, with a cushion to cover my time after filing. The more I thought about the fallout, extricating myself from this whole set of problems appealed compelling. I called Chad Wiseman.

"Sure, I can find someone to take the stones off your hands, but as I told you, you're going to be lucky to get half the value, a third of a million, for the stones. You're talking a whole different group of buyers. That'll take time. The broker'll take five per cent for arranging a sale."

"That sounds reasonable. Time's of the essence however. The estate needs the liquidity."

"I understand. I'll get back to you."

Susan Becker called my office that afternoon. "Hi, John. How are you?"

"I know that's a rhetorical question, but I'm doing fine now that you have taken over untangling the problems at Robertson Investments. What's up?"

"I know that you understand that we may become adversaries given the claims against Greg Robertson. Both the firm's clients and the firm itself may file claims against the estate in probate court. However, right now we have a mutual interest in getting our hands on the insurance proceeds. Sara and Greg's brothers do too, so I've contacted them to discuss how we fund a lawsuit against Alliance Insurance Company. I'll get court permission to pay half of the costs if the four of you will cover the other half pro rata. Shouldn't be a big expense proving whether Robertson was killed accidentally, was murdered or committed suicide. Only a jury can decide that, but they might end up flipping a coin given what you've told me."

"I'm happy to sign up for an eighth of the costs, but to be frank with you, as the claims against Robertson personally have mounted up, the estate might be short of funds."

"I understand, but the ranch is worth millions, and the firm's bankruptcy will allow it to have first claim on the proceeds of any ranch sale to pay litigation costs, so I'm okay."

"Good. Let's get it on with the insurance company."

• • •

For the first time in months, life returned to the normal slow pace that Blanco offered its residents. The city and county offer an unusual mosaic of Americana. The city of Blanco has grown over the years, ten per cent every decade, but the county has exploded, with elegant homes usually owned by retirees and near retirees. The county and the city have become more diverse, with the Hispanic population nearing thirty per cent. Many young couples move into the area to take advantage of the Blanco schools, where the average high school class is seventy rather than six hundred, as is true of Austin area urban schools. I liked the area, and as my practice progressed, I found myself handling more wills and estates than real estate and other disputes. I liked not having to be in court nearly as much.

Chad indeed sold the diamonds, but only for three hundred thousand, less than half what certified diamonds would go for. I didn't ask who bought them, but the money was wired into the estate account at Chase in Houston. That allowed me to bill to date and get paid, get Ben paid and, subject to later court approval if we filed bankruptcy, pay myself and Ben a modest advance against later fees. I held off filing the estate in bankruptcy for no good reason, knowing I'd eventually have to do that. Creditors weren't banging on my door, and claimants arising out of Robertson Investments would have to wait a long time to have a judge award them any money from the estate. There wouldn't be enough to make everyone whole, even with the ranch proceeds. I'd leave it to Sara and Linda Wilcox to sort out whether the ranch was separate or community property in the bankruptcy court.

I kept in touch with Sara, and like most widows, she bounced back from losing her husband and moved on. She told me she still sold jewelry to wealthy families and to Houston rappers, and I wondered whether she was the one who bought the uncertified diamonds Chad had sold for me. I didn't ask.

Spring migrated into early summer, replete with the heat. What's good about the hill country is that early in the morning and during the evening hours, the temperature goes down to a tolerable level. Carla and I spent hours on the gazebo both times.

Sal called two weeks after the bankruptcy, right after he got the official bankruptcy notice from the court. "John, I have to get those diamonds. Have they been released yet?" His call elevated my stress level back to April's level.

"Sorry, Sal. The diamonds were sold to pay estate creditors, subject to court approval later if title to the diamonds rested in the firm. You'll have to talk to Susan Becker, the lawyer for the firm, to get updates and find out how to file a claim. The estate is bankrupt too, and I'll have to file it into bankruptcy court this week. If the money for the diamonds did not come from the firm, but from other money Greg had, the proceeds from the diamond sales will be tied up in that bankruptcy. I'll let you know who to contact for that."

Sal exploded with a lengthy profane set of expletives, claiming I'd defrauded him. "My people will not be happy. Gonna hurt me personally and professionally. I don't know what I can do. You'll be hearing from them."

I couldn't tell whether Sal's statement threatened me, but I took it as such, remembering Smokey Hundley and his history. Then again, I stood on the periphery, and I had nothing to do with Paragon's loss of money. I told him I sympathized with him, told him I couldn't do anything. I emphasized that the probate and bankruptcy courts, along with the regulatory enforcement officers were keeping a close eye on everything that went on with Robertson and his firm. Finally I told him that anything he asked me to do would be unwound by court order. After he abruptly ended our call, I reveled in knowing that the bankruptcy filings would let me get rid of Paragon and Sal.

The mystery remained, though. Was Robertson killed or did he elaborately commit suicide?

# 18.

To answer the question, I needed to talk to Hal, and if he didn't have a ready answer, await the trial involving the insurance policy. And then the follow-up question. If someone murdered Greg, who did it and why?

Hal and I met at the Bean and Biscuit, the local coffee shop hangout. I brought him up to date on everything, and Hal remained silent for at least two minutes. Then he spoke.

"I've been through this before. Whenever there's a big problem, facts often point in opposite directions. Bad people get pissed when they figure they've been wronged. And that can lead to anything. The mob or cartel, or whoever is behind Paragon Diamonds, may have killed Greg, not only for screwing them out of a bunch of money but bringing the feds down on what sounds like a big blood diamond smuggling operation. There could be a bunch of people like Sara unknowingly funneling diamonds into the stream of commerce. Hundley could be their designated hitter who orchestrated Greg's death, but he could also be a hired hand retained simply to recover as much money as he could, including the diamonds. With enough money any organization can arrange a hit."

"Yeah, my criminal defense lawyer friend, Bob Rivera, tells me that the street quote for killing someone in Houston is only twenty grand. He says the drug runners are staggered in their runs from Mexico and get bored, so they do hits for entertainment between runs. Scary."

"On the other hand, Robertson may have committed suicide. Look where he was. Nothing he did worked out; in fact he made things worse financially. He knew the game was up, and seeing Madoff go to jail with a life term must have made an impression on him. So he might have simply decided to commit suicide in a way that appeared to be an accident, for two reasons. First and foremost, an accident would somewhat salvage his reputation, he may have thought. And as important, the six million he left his brothers and Sara made a nice good-by present."

"We're still missing facts here. Whether murder or suicide, third parties had to be involved in fixing the plane to run out of fuel and crash. If Greg committed suicide, why would he go to the trouble of manipulating the fuel gauge, for instance?"

"So that the authorities, if they dug deeply into what went on, would conclude that someone murdered him. Anything to take the spotlight off suicide."

"How does this get resolved then?"

"May not be. May not matter, actually, for what you're involved in."

"What do you mean?"

"The authorities care whether Greg committed suicide or was murdered. That's their job. The only issue relevant to the firm and to the estate is the insurance policy. Given where Robertson's estate stands right now, I'd pack it in and file the estate in bankruptcy and wash my hands of this, except of course, to help the bankruptcy trustee sell the ranch."

Wise words, but as Carla admonished me when I told her about my meeting with Hal, I hate to give up on puzzles. I was happy to reach a conclusion and told Carla, "I think that Hal and you are right to tell me to file the estate in bankruptcy. I'll tend to that and then as executor simply watch this roll out, as a spectator. Thanks for clarifying everything."

That cinched it. I'd have Linda Wilcox file the estate in bankruptcy tomorrow.

● ● ●

Before I got that done, I decided to warn a bunch of people that the estate would be filing in bankruptcy. I began with Stonewater. He needed to know that I'd be quitting the field. As usual he answered my call.

"I've been meaning to call you. Our investigation has broadened a bit, and we may have found out how the crash was orchestrated. The analysis of the altered fuel gauge told us that someone programmed it to go down half as fast as a normal gauge would show. We're beginning to think that the sabotage began at the hanger in Houston, at the base operator. When Greg took off from Houston, we think the gauge showed near full, when in fact the fuel tanks were really only sixty per cent full. He burned up most of what was left in the flight to the ranch, so when he returned, while the gauge showed half full, the tank actually held less than an eighth. The rest you know."

"So the question remains: Who altered the fuel gauge and why, correct?"

"Correct, but we went a little further. We got back with HondaJet and asked them what they'd done to the plane when their personnel visited the hanger two weeks prior to the fatal trip. That's led to a real mystery. HondaJet says they haven't serviced Greg's plane since the hundred hour checkup they made six months before the crash. The operator insists that a tank truck with the HondaJet logo came to service the aircraft a week before the accident, and two men in white uniforms with HondaJet logos on the uniforms stayed two hours. Once we talked to the operator, they said they did wonder why the company had sent a truck with a tank on it. We're trying to figure out who those guys were and who put them up to it."

"Should I tell Sara about this?"

"I'd wait a while, frankly. She's still a person of interest, and I want to be the one to tell her and see what her reaction is."

"Not what I was expecting. The reason I called got lost in this. I need to tell you that I'm going to file the estate in Chapter 7 bankruptcy tomorrow. Every indication points to there being way more liabilities than assets because of Greg's financial manipulations at the firm. Linda Wilcox, the bankruptcy lawyer for the estate, suggested that I file a bare-bones Chapter 7 with little information and then let the trustee, whoever he or she is, fill in the blanks. Of course I'll be helping her."

"That doesn't surprise me, knowing what I know from you and the SEC investigation."

"What's next?"

"We'd like to interview Sara, but she's got a good lawyer, and so far they've resisted talking to us." I didn't tell Oliver that I'd been the one who'd referred Bob Rivera to Sara.

"Understandable."

"Other things are going on. The New York office is digging into Paragon Diamonds from that end. We need to know who's in charge there and who owns the business. At a minimum they're flouting the customs duties. That's enough to bring charges, but I'm sure the guys there want to charge the kingpins."

"I'll make sure that you're on the notice list when I file the bankruptcy. Thanks for the update. My sense is that you're getting closer to figuring this out."

"Not sure of that. We won't know that until we get to the end."

I hoped that letting other parties know about the estate bankruptcy filing wouldn't take as long as the call to Stonewater did. I knew that Grainger and Grainger had to be next. Susan Becker, now in charge of the Robertson firm's filing answered, and I told her why I'd called.

"I've been expecting the filing. Every day, when I come in there are additional filings against the firm by clients who've been victimized. Once it's filed for the estate, you'll be done. There's an automatic monitoring service that'll tell Linda who the trustee is. As soon as one is appointed she'll let you know."

Next was my team at Robertson Investments. The calls weren't long. Paul and Rose both sounded fatigued and even angry at their deceased leader. So did Rob. Finally, I called Sal at Paragon Diamonds, if only to keep Hundley away from me. He didn't answer his cell phone so I was happy to leave a message.

I called Sara, knowing that no one had short conversations with her. "Sara, we've been expecting this, I suppose, but I need to file Greg's estate in bankruptcy. There are too many claims against Greg for me and the estate to handle. Sorting out the claims will be a time-consuming effort. You'll need one more lawyer, a lawyer who knows bankruptcy law, to represent you in that. The big issue is whether the ranch is half yours through community property or Greg's separate property. Creditors will want all of the proceeds when it's sold, not half. The bankruptcy will allow the estate to deliver clean title to the ranch. With the claims pending against the estate, no right-minded person would be willing to buy it right now."

"Thank God that I have my business, but Greg's death and the stories coming out are hurting my jewelry sales. The media love big stories about one of the city's big financial gurus dying and then a bunch of alleged wrongdoing coming out. I've got more inventory than I need right now, but I was able to buy a number of diamonds recently from a Chicago diamond broker at a nice discount."

"Did they have a country of origin warranty or were they Kimberley certified?"

"I don't know. No one asks. They're in separate little bags with the details of each stone written on each bag. Doesn't say who sold them or where they came from."

"Okay. I'll keep you up to date from here on. Have your bankruptcy lawyer call me to coordinate sorting out the assets."

"Greg gave me three million a year ago. Is there a problem with that?"

"Your lawyer will have to address that. I don't know bankruptcy law well, but anything within a year can be questioned, and the burden of proof that a transfer after that was designed to hurt creditors is a high bar."

"I wish we could get through this and have it over. It's enough losing Greg and now this. We'll talk later."

I went home early that day. The two bankruptcy filings promised to lift a big cloud that had been hanging over me for the past three months. I felt my schedule clearing and hoped that my normal, slow-paced life would resume.

# 19.

A quiet life was not to be, however. Stonewater called the next morning. Early and on my cell phone.

"Sorry to bother you so early, but I wanted you to know. My New York office called to tell me that Sal Minardi turned up this morning. Dead, killed execution style. A worker found him right in the heart of the diamond district, in an alley off 47th street between Fifth and Sixth Avenues. Whoever runs Paragon Diamonds doesn't mess around."

"If Paragon arranged Greg's murder, Sal would be in the know. Do you think they killed him because he might squeal or because Greg's firm lost Paragon a bundle of money?"

"None of us know anything right now, but I'd think for both reasons. Someone above him must have dug into the facts about Paragon's money and realized they had a dead loss on their hands."

"Do you think I'm in any danger?"

"Whether it's the mob or a cartel, they're not terrorists. They're particular who they take out and know that enforcement officials are less concerned when they rub out one of their own rather than an innocent bystander, especially if the bystander's a lawyer."

I laughed. I needed the relief. Stonewater continued. "Of course, you should always take care. They might not be aware that you couldn't have legally turned over the diamonds to them." My concerns returned.

"Oh, one more thing, John. We re-interviewed the manager of the base operator in Houston. Lewis Aviation Services. Still can't unlock the mystery about the people wearing HondaJet uniforms, the ones we think tampered with the fuel gauge module and drained the tanks. Their security scanners are on a seventy-two hour loop, so they're no help. The descriptions of the two men are plain vanilla. The descriptions fit half the male population between the ages of twenty-five and forty. Not Hundley anyway, so we have a dead end there. One thing the manager mentioned, though, was that Robertson was really into his aircraft, and he even got both a hard copy and an electronic copy of the specifications manual and maintenance manual for the plane. The latter explains how to open the cowl in front of the plane to access the dashboard from behind, as well as the control mechanisms, both foot and steering wheels. The death investigation for Robertson is still open, and his having access to that information tilts things back a bit toward suicide."

"Interesting. I didn't think of Greg that way. He seemed so into his financial dealings that I figured he had no other outside interests. We need to get the cause of death wrapped up. I'll see what I can do."

"Thanks. Keep me aware of anything going on from your end and with the proceedings in Houston."

"I will."

Linda Wilcox had called while I was talking to Stonewater, so I called her back. "I called to tell you that the trustee for the estate is Elaine Fairchild. She's a solo practitioner with plenty of experience. I work well with her, and I'll suggest to Susan Becker and Elaine that we consolidate the two bankruptcies since there are so many intertwined liabilities." She sounded competent and was all business. None of the chitchat that preceded most Hill Country conversations. She sent me a list of what she'd be needing and said she'd made a "barebones" filing to get things started–the detailed list of assets and liabilities could come later. I got to work on that and thought how wise I was to take an advance before the filing.

• • •

I wanted out, but my continuing as the executor of Greg's estate kept me involved and worried. I could resign, of course, but the judge might not allow me to do that since I'd signed on to begin with, and Greg's brothers both lived outside of Texas. What everyone involved needed was a determination of the cause of death so that the insurance policy could be settled one way or another. That would allow the two bankruptcies to grind their way forward sorting out who got what. That would take several years at least, judging by the seven year journey that the Madoff bankruptcy took.

No inquest had been held relating to Greg's death. The coroner in Lee county, where the crash occurred east of Austin, didn't want any part of a controversy and ruled the death an accident without any real investigation. At the time, no one had any hint of Greg's troubles, so I understood the coroner's ruling.

I hate to do legal research. It's like crossword puzzles, which I also avoid. Nonetheless, I had the idea that the parties might use an inquest procedure to determine the cause of death, that is, whether suicide or murder. The crash was no accident. I floated the idea with Linda Wilcox, Bruce Silverton, Elaine Fairchild and Susan Becker, the attorneys in charge of the two bankruptcies, on a conference call.

Susan was the first to respond. "I can't speak for Bruce, but anything that simplifies both proceedings has to be good. What exactly do you have in mind?"

"I'd try to get the insurance company and the interested parties to agree to a formal inquest hearing. Really an arbitration. If you haven't done one of those recently, it's like an ordinary trial. Most parties want to make it an informal hearing rather than a formal one where the rules of evidence are invoked. If the insurance company wants to use a jury, we could do that too. The hearing would be under our state arbitration law, so that whoever hears the evidence and makes a decision will be making a final determination.

"Then we'd call the people who are in the know to testify, starting with Oliver Stonewater, who's in charge of the FBI investigation. I suppose we'd have someone, Rob Hall for instance, describe the state of the financial affairs at Robertson Investments at the time of the crash. I don't know who would testify about Paragon Diamonds, perhaps Stonewater. I'd testify regarding my dealings with Greg, his state of mind, Hundley, and my meetings with Greg, especially for the codicil. Sara and Rose could give their impressions of Greg's state of mind right before the crash too. The important thing will be to get everyone on board to accepting the determination at the hearing as final."

"I'm not sure whether this is brilliant or unworkable," Becker said. "The benefit of doing this is clear. It'll shorten the time consumed sitting in bankruptcy court with these two cases and allow us to figure out who gets the proceeds. May be the beneficiaries but we'll be fighting for the creditors.

"The same evidence would be presented in litigation with the insurance company, but litigating the cause of death in a regular court would literally take years. Knowing how litigators are these days, they'd burn up tens of thousands of dollars going over well-trod ground. I think the cost-benefit of most depositions is quite negative. Let's go for it. I'm sure somebody will pop up and oppose the idea, claiming that new facts are sure to come out down the road. Worth the try anyway."

"Good," I said. "If you two will figure out what permissions we need from each of the courts, I'll contact the insurance company and the beneficiaries and try to get them on board. If they won't agree, we may still want to have an inquest. The determination there would weigh heavily on any later litigation, so the insurer might settle out after the inquest even if they were not a part of it."

Elaine spoke up. "Who's going to pay for this?"

"Good question. I'm thinking that each party should pay their own part. My fee would come out of the estate, since I am most interested in a determination of the cause of death. I need to know who the real beneficiaries of the estate should be. I doubt the brothers had anything to do with Greg's death, but if they were, they'd be disqualified as beneficiaries. I'd orchestrate the

proceeding and put evidence on, but you guys and the beneficiaries would also be permitted to present your own evidence
and witnesses."

"Just so we don't run up big bills for the bankruptcy court,"
Elaine said. "We'll see. The benefit of closing the death and insurance issue gets my vote to try, even if the insurance company
won't buy in."

"Great. I'll move forward."

The key to the hearing resolving the cause of death issue
would be the government witnesses, Pat Carnegie for the NTSB
and Oliver Stonewater for the FBI. I wouldn't think the participants would want a jury, but we'd need a judge. Fortunately, I
thought of a crusty, retired Houston federal judge, Joe Wiseman,
to preside. Before I talked to him I had to line up the witnesses. I
called Stonewater.

"Hi, John. How can I help you?"

I explained the state of affairs in the two bankruptcies, ending
with the one unsolved mystery, the cause of death. Then I asked
whether he could take time out to tell a hearing what he knew.

"I'd have to get permission, and of course, the powers that be
here will want a transcript to make sure I haven't screwed up. I think
they'll agree. Actually, this is fast becoming a cold case, although
not much time has passed. If Robertson was murdered, the killers
have covered their tracks well. The Paragon Diamonds office has
closed, and their mail is going to a drop box, you know, the mail-
boxes they have at copy centers. We've tracked the two LLCs who
had money at Robertson Investments, thinking that somehow they
were connected with Paragon, Hundley and the diamonds. A dead-
end there. The owner of the LLCs is a Panamanian anonymous

entity. The individuals there are straw men who get paid to do whatever anonymously. So far no clues as to who's behind Minardi's murder according to my New York cohorts. The modification of the fuel module has also led to a dead end. Perhaps a hearing will trigger a new avenue or approach. At a minimum, though, if we do have that hearing, it'll create a record of where the case stands for anyone looking at it in the future."

"You mentioned Hundley. I wonder where he is."

"No telling, but we can find him. He's not one to go underground. We should interview him. We can force him in. Might do that at the same time as the hearing to get it done at once."

"Good. I'll call Pat Carnegie at the NTSB and make sure that he'll participate."

"Let me know if you have any trouble in that regard. I'll help enlist him if he's reluctant. They released the final report a while ago, so that's public information now."

"Great. I'll let you know once I've got everybody lined up."

# 20.

Next on my list was Judge Joseph Wiseman. Took a while to run him down, but a friendly person in the federal court office in Houston reluctantly gave me his contact information after I explained what I was calling for.

"Judge Wiseman, this is John Mariner. I'm an attorney but acting right now as the executor of the estate of Gregory Robertson."

"I'm surprised. His name's been all over the papers and TV here, including the bankruptcy of the firm. Quite a Ponzi scheme, it turns out. But what in the world are you calling me for? I thought you were living a bucolic life in Blanco county."

"I am, or rather was until I got involved with the Robertson family. Greg had a ranch up here and I was his local lawyer." I explained the basic facts and the six million dollar insurance policy, ending with the question of the cause of death. Then I went over my idea for a sort of inquest, an administrative hearing to determine, as best we could, whether Greg was murdered or committed suicide.

"That's intriguing. To tell you the truth, since I retired, I've continued to judge cases as a retired judge. The federal docket here is so crowded lawyers will agree to a substitute judge to make things move along. The first order of business is a date. How long do you think this will take?"

"Assuming no jury and no one invoking the formal rules of evidence, no longer than a week. I thought we might begin on a Monday morning and go till finished, hopefully less than a week. Then you can take a week or two to review what's been testified to and issue a ruling."

"Okay, I'll do it. I'll let you know what I'll charge. There'll also be a separate charge for support services in addition to the court reporter. I'll need someone to type up my findings, for instance. In looking at my schedule, the best I can do is a month from now, the second week in July. Does that work?"

"I'll have to check with the key witnesses first and then line up the other ones representing the parties in interest. As to your charges, if you'll figure out what a total cost looks like, I'll get the participants to kick in their part before the hearing. Don't want payment to be a problem for this."

Wiseman laughed. "Don't know why, with two bankrupt entities, a widow and a bunch of government people involved. Thanks for thinking through that."

"Stay tuned." With the judge lined up, I then called Stonewater and Carnegie, and they agreed to the date since it was a month away. Then I got Sara and Greg's brothers on board—they had no forewarning what I was up to prior to the calls to them. While surprised, they wanted resolution so they could move on, and while the insurance proceeds were substantial, none of them really needed the money. Next I had to get Rob Hall scheduled to outline the financial schemes and dealings and then Paul and Rose to give their impressions of Greg, his habits, and how he was acting right before the crash. I'd have to testify about the diamonds and Greg's state of mind. Maybe we could drag Hundley in if we could find him. I got pumped planning the hearing and the final resolution the hearing would bring to all parties.

"Hey, John," Rob said. "Been meaning to call you. First to thank you for getting me involved in the Robertson Investments. It'll be quite a gravy train for me, and I like forensic accounting better than anything."

I brought Rob up to date on my plan to have a hearing on the cause of death to clear the issue of the insurance policy, asking him to confirm that he could be a witness at the hearing the second week of July.

"Let me take a quick look at my calendar." He paused. "Hard for me to clear a week, but I think I can move the two appointments I already have. Book it."

"Thanks."

Rob continued. "I need to bring you up to date on one more thing. Susan Becker had me take a look at Greg's accounts at the firm and his personal accounts to see whether any clues popped up. You were smart to file the estate in bankruptcy. Robertson didn't appear to see a bright line between the firm and himself when it came down to cash. On three or four occasions a year, he'd take money out of the firm and put the cash into his own accounts. He had an account at a small bank in, of all places, Ozona, Texas. We checked the history of that account, and Greg wrote a large check the same day that he first asked you for a meeting, the one that led to the codicil. The large check went to a New York firm that buys and sells bitcoins. Based on the date of the check and the market for those things, he bought one hundred fifty of them, worth over three quarters of a million. We're still trying to locate and access his bitcoin account to see whether there's anything left in it. First we'll need his password. Haven't found any detail written down describing the account anywhere."

"I don't know much about bitcoins. Is there a place I can go to find out the details and history of disbursement from the bitcoin account?"

"No, it's totally anonymous if you want it to be. Robertson must have written down the information somewhere. Too much money to risk forgetting the account number and password."

"I'll see what his wallet had in it. No trace of a password for that in the papers you and I have seen. If he wanted to buy, say, a fuel module from an anonymous source, that might be the way."

"Bingo. Hypothetical at this point. Having seen where he and the firm were when he bought the coins, he may have been establishing a getaway fund he could use in a place like Indonesia where he could stay undercover. Knowing him, however, the bitcoins would only last a year or so even as cheap as things are down there."

"Here's hoping we find a pot of gold at the end of that rainbow."

Rob laughed and signed off. I spent the rest of the day lining up the insurance company, Susan Becker and her firm, Bruce Silverton, Linda Wilcox, Elaine Fairchild, and Sara and her brothers-in-law. As I talked to each one, I found explaining my idea easier not as an inquest but as a simple arbitration process, where the parties agreed to be bound by the determination of the arbitrator. The law is strongly in favor of arbitration; decisions are enforced unless there is "manifest disregard for the law or the facts," with a strong presumption in favor of the arbitrator's fact findings. My role would be that of laying out the facts through Stonewater, Rob and others, then allowing the rest of the attendees to add to what the witnesses—primarily Carnegie, Stonewater, Rob and Rose—testified to. I let Judge Wiseman set up the place for the hearing and the retention of the court reporter.

Not inappropriately, Wiseman chose the large conference room at the firm for the hearing. That was the only place that could hold everyone, and since the firm had been downsized, each side and each witness could have their own little office to prepare and confer privately.

I'm more of an introvert than an extrovert, and talking on the phone the better part of the day tired me so much that at four, I packed it in and went home. The three kids were happy to see me but even happier that they'd been dismissed from the last day of the school year. Wild Indians. I gathered Carla and a few snacks, along with a bottle of good malbec, and adjourned to the gazebo, my favorite lounging place. Summer had arrived. The temperature was around 85, but the nice breeze made lounging comfortable outside. I brought Carla up to date with everything. Unusually, she took in everything I said, not offering any comment or opinion.

"I think you're going in the right direction, John. Maybe this will close everything out and you can get back to your usual routine. Given the facts, I'd hate to be Judge Wiseman. Which way to go, murder or suicide, isn't clear. Certainly not beyond a reasonable doubt."

"Judge Wiseman's standard will be the one we use in civil trials. A preponderance of the evidence. That means fifty per cent or more. Not sure even that standard can be met."

"You've been so involved in the Robertson death you've ignored other problems. Did they ever find out who torched the equipment at PK's?"

"Interesting that you asked. No, no sign of who did that, but the protests have continued. Like that pipeline in North Dakota. The protestors claimed that Goliath is bringing oak wilt to our area. That didn't work, so now they're claiming that the pipe itself is defective since it's been out in the weather for close to a year. Goliath has marshalled and stored miles and miles of pipes, as you know, and as new delays have come up, they've been unable to complete the line through the hill country. At least Goliath is furnishing employment for a number of locals around here, especially enforcement officers. I'd go crazy if I had to sit in a car all day, even if they paid me fifteen bucks an hour."

Carla giggled. "You can't even sit still for a half hour. By the way a big package came from UPS for you today."

"I wonder what it is. Haven't ordered anything online recently." I went in to retrieve the package and brought it back to the gazebo. I opened it and there it was—Greg Robertson's laptop. No sender listed.

• • •

I looked forward to the hearing, but meanwhile I returned to my normal vocation helping locals out with legal matters and sorting out city problems. For instance, I'd ignored a little problem close to home. Needed and update. A church member called to report that a man was sleeping inside the unlocked church every night. I called Tom Maynor, and one of his deputies rousted the guy out of the church, telling him that he'd be arrested if he went back in. Trespass. I went to the church to make sure that the worship area was in order, and I discovered that he'd signed the visitor book "Jesus of Nazareth." Tom called a few days later.

"John, we've followed the guy during the day. He shows up at the food bank promptly when it opens, gets food for the day, and then he walks over to the town library, where there's wifi. He spends the whole day there sitting on one of the outside benches. The people at the food bank and library don't want us running him out of town, feeling that he's a person in need. We've identified him and he doesn't have any criminal record that we can find. Does the municipal league or anyone have any guidelines advising how to treat these people?"

"I don't think so. It's a big problem for cities, especially the big ones in a temperate climate. I'd keep watching him and ticket him if he gets out of line. He shouldn't be treated differently than any other citizen."

"Agreed. But he's not mentally all there. Let me know if you find anything."

I got on the internet to find background material on the explosion of homeless in the United States. No single explanation of the epidemic. I let the matter rest to see what else would happen. But I did migrate to the guy's website, whose URL the food bank manager had passed on to the chief, and the website made clear that our friend was not mentally healthy, a schizophrenic. The non-violent kind. I heard nothing for two weeks and forgot the homeless issue as I prepared for the hearing, but I knew the problem wasn't going away.

# 21.

I drove to Houston leisurely the day before our hearing at Robertson Investments. My primary motivation in getting prepared was simple. I did not want to do a sloppy job in front of my peers—Judge Wiseman, Rob, Stonewater and Carnegie—out of personal pride in my lawyer skills. The others too. Who knows; someday I might have to go back to Houston. The final decision on Greg's death would get the entire tangled episode over, at least for me. My opinion about Greg's death wasn't really important. I switched back and forth between murder and suicide. Today I tended to think murder, since the headlines reported yet another assassination in London, of a Russian former accountant who criticized not only Putin but the oligarchs and their kleptocracy. The guy was done in by the identical methods used on Sal. Murdered brutally to send a message.

I had my legal pad ready to guide me and keep the presentation orderly, but now legal pads are on laptops. Over the past three weeks I'd made a list of questions for each witness. The sequence of witnesses to testify would drive understanding. I couldn't decide whether to put witnesses on first to introduce

Greg and his mental state or to simply start with the crash and move from there. I decided the latter. I'd prepared as well as I could, and the next morning had my adrenaline pulsing. Secretly I enjoyed what I was doing.

The Robertson Investments conference room sat in the corner of the building floor, twenty feet by sixty. The conference table was large enough for a meeting of the President's cabinet and held chairs sufficient for the fifteen participants. Wiseman would sit in the middle of the table looking out. The witnesses would sit across from him, looking in so that they would not be distracted by the outside. The court reporter sat next to the judge and had set up a large screen that would show the witness testifying, with a streaming transcription of the testimony. How technology had changed transcriptions. I remember the days, not long ago, when an accelerated transcription of testimony meant a day or two.

I got there early to insure that I was prepared to greet Judge Wiseman when he arrived. Rose and Paul had already arrived and had begun preparing the room for a long haul with coffee, drinks and even doughnuts. I wasn't hungry, as you might suspect. Wiseman arrived, reviewed the preparations, and after approving same took coffee and sat down in his chair.

"I'd like to wait until all the parties in interest have arrived so that I can set the stage for this hearing," the judge said.

"Good idea." That gave me time to have another cup of coffee, collect my thoughts, and review my notes. As people arrived, greetings were exchanged. Many had heard about the other participants but had not met them, and I enjoyed seeing the reactions as each new arrival got introduced and the others in the room took the measure of each new arrival. There's something magic in human interaction that can't be conveyed over a telephone call, even Facetime or Zoom.

Besides Sara, Rose, Paul, Rob and Pat Carnegie, two people from the insurance company— an executive-looking guy and a lawyer— came in after the others had arrived. Both looked serious and humorless. Of course, six million of insurance money was at stake. Susan Becker, Bruce Silverton, Linda Wilcox and Elaine Fairchild, representing the two bankrupt entities, came as a group. Bruce is an attorney too. Those bankruptcy lawyers stick together. Finally, Stonewater arrived. The assembled group sat around the immense table. I had already grabbed the chair to the right of Judge Wiseman and had Rob sit next to me. Stonewater and Carnegie sat next to the witness chair opposite the judge. The rest scattered around the table.

"Let's get started, everyone. I'm Joe Wiseman and will be presiding today, as you know. Let's get the preliminaries out of the way. I understand that Mariner has circulated an arbitration agreement pursuant to which each of the parties in interest, particularly the insurance company and the beneficiaries, have agreed to be bound by determination of the cause of death. Is that correct?"

All of us nodded our heads. Wiseman continued. "Please sign the arbitration agreement if you have not done so already. The court reporter to my left, Stephanie Clodt, will record your testimony, both the video and the verbal testimony. From time to time she may interrupt the witness to clarify the words. If you are going to testify, please speak up and speak clearly so that the automated transcription can work best. At a normal trial, witnesses are excluded from the courtroom so that their testimony won't be affected by the testimony of others. In this case, as I understand from Mr. Mariner, there's going to be little testimony that overlaps or conflicts, so you can remain in the room.

"Similarly, a normal trial imposes strict rules of evidence. For instance, I'm sure everyone has heard that evidence based on hearsay can't be admitted in evidence. Both because this is an informal proceeding and because there's no jury, I won't enforce the normal rules of evidence unless someone objects. The theory at least is that I can weigh the veracity of any hearsay or unsubstantiated recitation of facts. Does anyone object to the manner of the proceeding as I've related?"

The room was silent. "Good. Let's get started then."

The judge called for the first witness, looking at me directly. I began with Pat Carnegie. My job would be easier than a normal trial. I'd first get the witness to identify himself or herself and state his or her relationship to the incidents. Then I'd ask a broad question to allow the witness to tell his story unimpeded. I did that with Carnegie, and he reviewed in detail the reason for the plane going down. I asked whether he discovered evidence of wrongdoing, and he testified that the fuel module in the plane wasn't original, that it had been reprogrammed to show less decline as fuel was consumed, with the result that the plane ran out of gas on the return to Houston. Judge Wiseman asked for detail regarding where the replaced module had been purchased, and Carnegie told Wiseman what he knew, that the module had been purchased through intermediaries that couldn't be identified, entities who wanted to insure anonymity. Then Carnegie turned to the way that the plane had been modified, saying that the investigators initially presumed that the alteration and extraction of the fuel occurred at the deceased's ranch. Later the investigation turned to the Houston home base of the aircraft, and Carnegie related the odd and unidentified visit of the truck a week before the incident. Wiseman's final question: "In your experience, do you have any idea whether the deceased or any other party involved with him had the knowledge and experience to conjure up this module modification?"

"No sir. I'm here in part to hear the testimony in the hopes that we can answer that question and I can close my investigation."

I called Oliver Stonewater next. His investigation stood at the core of the death issue. Like Carnegie, I identified him, asked his position and what part he played in the inquiry. Stonewater came on as a knowledgeable, competent and articulate storyteller, so I again simply asked a broad question, namely how he got involved and what he had discovered.

"This case befuddles me. Let me lay this out as best I can, but feel free to interrupt if you have questions if I'm not clear. We're here to decide whether Robertson committed suicide or whether he was murdered. Let's look at what we know.

"Robertson may have been murdered. Mr. Hall will testify in detail, but both Robertson Investments and the estate of Gregory Robertson are in bankruptcy because, it seems, Greg ran a Ponzi scheme, promising investors a stable return in good times or bad. Because of bad trades and a number of investors wanting out, the firm increasingly lost liquidity and Robertson scrambled to keep matters afloat. Prior to his death, based on emails and phone voicemails, a number of angry investors assaulted him verbally, demanding information and asking for their money back. Two in particular stand out. Paragon Diamonds had an eight figure investment at the firm, and they've claimed he personally bought diamonds and didn't pay for them. The investment money came in by wire, so the firm wasn't taking cash or money orders. Suspicious nonetheless. The other suspicious accounts are two Panamanian LLCs. Susan Becker will testify about those entities, but so far we can't find anyone home there. The manager is a straw man running anonymous entities, connected to a law firm down there. Almost impossible to get anyone charged with wire fraud down there. No word from them, which makes us think that either the money belongs to Paragon or to another person or other entity that wants to remain anonymous. We're beginning to think that the investments were made by Paragon Diamonds as a part of a money-laundering scheme, sponsored by the Mafia or by one of the cartels."

The assembled group listened intently as Stonewater continued. "There are additional pointers here. First, the complexity of arranging the engineered plane crash had to be the work of a sophisticated organization, not the work of one man. Designing the way Robertson was to die and then pulling off the module substitution and draining the fuel tanks had to involve multiple parties. Second, as Mr. Mariner will testify, a man named Bart Hundley lurked around Blanco for a great deal of time. He must have worked for Paragon. This is a man quite capable of heading up any plan to kill Robertson. We have him in custody in Florida for a minor offense and we could bring him here if you'd like. He says he worked for Paragon and only was retained to recover diamonds Robertson bought from Paragon and didn't pay for.

"At any rate, if my instincts are correct, when the mob or cartel saw that they were going to lose big money and that Paragon's illicit money-laundering operation might be exposed publicly, getting rid of Robertson made sense to them, both to silence any knowledge he had of who was behind the entities and as retribution for losing their money.

"On the other hand, let's assume a suicide. Robertson was boxed in at the end and had nowhere to go. The firm was functionally bankrupt. He must have seen that ahead of him was a ruined career and reputation. His personal life wasn't any better. As Sara Robertson will tell you, the marital relationship was on the rocks. Assuming he was aware of what we now know, what would he do? He had to consider the six million dollar policy, but he knew that the policy would be cancelled if he committed suicide. The incontestability clause wouldn't run out until the end of a year, which was over eight months away. So he decided to make his death look like an accident. Pat Carnegie tells me that they went through the personal effects he had with him on the aircraft. Among the items was a prescription for hydrocodone. Ten milligram pills, the strongest you can get. The hydrocodone showed up on him at the autopsy. Hard to tell how much, but it'd make sense that he wanted to partially anesthetize himself for the crash. Two more things that bolster this theory. Robertson diverted a small sum, for him, eight hundred thousand, from the firm to buy bitcoins. Why did he do that? Possibly to be able to buy a fuel module anonymously. However, that would cost no more than five grand. Another explanation for his buying bitcoins was that the coins would fund his escape hatch, that he could run away somewhere and spend the bitcoins to live on until people forgot him. Which brings us back to the murder theory."

"Interesting," Judge Wiseman said. "You've been closer to this death than anyone. Murder or suicide?"

"I don't know. I'm here to find out what you think. I lean slightly toward the murder theory."

# 22.

The day wore on. The testimony took up much of the day, since those attending often asked questions of each other that led to more testimony. Had to break periodically and took an hour for lunch, all of us going our own ways. Judge Wiseman made clear that he wanted the hearing to move quickly. By four that afternoon, though, he was ready to adjourn. Being in his late seventies, I understood how the constancy of the testimony tired him out, as it did with the rest of us. I retreated to my hotel room at the Lancaster to review my notes, read the Wall Street Journal and relax. I called Carla and brought her up to date. I'd wanted her to come to the hearing, but with three kids to look after, she had no alternative but to stay home.

Tom Maynor had left a voice mail, asking me to call but told me it was not urgent. I called.

"Hey, Tom. What's up?"

"I wanted you to know that the homeless situation here has cleared up. Long story but the essentials are that I personally found the guy and talked to him. Got his real name and ran a check on him. Mostly minor violations, but a few breaking and entering charges that were dismissed on the condition that he got evaluated mentally. I called and got a place for him at the Harbor Shelter in San Antonio. Great safe place. Our friend didn't want to go to any shelter, however. Said shelters were dangerous. A day later one of my deputies found an unoccupied house that had been entered. Kind of thing I would expect from our guy. Nothing damaged. Whoever it was made a clear attempt to straighten things. Without accusing him of doing it, I confronted him and told him that breaking and entering would not be tolerated. That the offense was a felony that could get someone a couple of years in prison. That's the last I've heard of him. I checked his website this evening, and he said he'd taken up residence along the beach at Surfside, near Freeport. Now he can break into unoccupied beach houses there with impunity. I'll let the police there know. But Blanco is thankfully rid of him."

"A good solution for the town. I hope you told the mayor. That kind of guy should be in an institution somewhere."

"Yeah, but the law no longer allows involuntary stays."

"Sad." We think that every problem has a solution, but there are plenty of insoluble problems in human society. Homelessness is one of them.

● ● ●

Judge Wiseman began the Tuesday session promptly at nine. "Okay. Mr. Mariner, who's next?"

"I'll have Rose Mendoza testify so that you can get a better sense of Greg Robertson and his mental state right before his death."

I asked Rose to take the witness chair. I could see that she was nervous, as anyone would have been under the circumstances. The reporter swore her in as she took her seat. As with the other witnesses, I began by having her tell who she was and what her position was at the firm.

"Rose, please tell us what you did at Robertson Investments, including the length of time you worked directly for Mr. Robertson."

"I've been Greg's executive secretary for ten years. He hired me from one of our competitors after I'd worked in the back office of that company after college. Greg told me that another employee at the firm had recommended me. Greg had an unusual personality. Since he was proficient with the computer, he had little need for me to do letters, emails, and spreadsheets for him, so I also worked for Paul Streeter." Paul nodded.

"Did you see Mr. Robertson in a social context?"

"No, except at the firm Christmas party. Since I'm married with two kids, I've always been anxious to get home after work. I knew that Greg hung out with his traders occasionally after work."

"I see you brought a letter with the firm letterhead. What's that?"

"I didn't know what to do with this, but last Friday I cleaned out Greg's desk. In the back of the bottom right drawer, I found this letter in an envelope that said 'For Rose or Paul in the event of my demise.' I knew we were going to do this today, so I brought it with me. I couldn't sleep over the weekend."

"Would you read the letter to us?"

"Sure. Here it is. 'Rose and Paul, I assume that you've opened this because I have died. I have been under severe financial distress, as you have discovered since my death. I am truly sorry for getting you two, Sara and my investors into an irretrievably bad financial situation. The worst thing is that I have received serious death threats from several people. One's from Sal Minardi of Paragon Diamonds, and another claims to be the head of the company that owns the two Panamanian LLCs. If something happens to me, please have the police fully investigate my death as a murder in retribution for my losing those people so much money. The police will find that none of them are good people and quite capable of violence.' It's signed 'Greg'."

"That's quite a letter," Judge Wiseman said. "Let's take a break."

●●●

After fifteen minutes, Wiseman called us back to resume our hearing. The lawyer for the insurance company interrupted. "Judge, may I comment on the letter?"

"Sure. Proceed. We're informal here."

"We've been thinking. I want to point out to you that while the letter may express a legitimate concern that harm might come to him, Mr. Robertson may have orchestrated his death by suicide in a deliberate manner. Mr. Stonewater has already testified that Robertson could have arranged for the plane to be tampered with, and given that, could have prepared this letter as a further means of diverting investigators from the possibility of suicide. The letter can be viewed two ways."

"Thank you for that observation. Very astute. I'll keep that in mind."

"All right. Mr. Mariner, please proceed."

"Now try to think back to the two weeks prior to Greg's death. How did he act? Do you have a sense of his mental state?"

"Hindsight's always twenty-twenty, they say. Same for me. Greg's personality changed over time as the firm's position changed. I now know how our finances deteriorated over the last year. His wife Sara and I talked at least once a week, in part to coordinate Greg's schedule. I did his travel arrangements, for instance. Sara complained how grumpy Greg got before his death, and I noticed that he seemed always on edge. Of course, the markets had taken a dip then, so I wrote off his anxiety as a reaction to the market volatility. Everyone was a bit edgy."

"Anything unusual the week before Greg went to his ranch the last time?"

"Not really. He appeared happy to go up to his ranch to arrange a cattle sale. Helped get his mind off business. He didn't talk to me much like he used to a year or two before his death. For instance, before, he often asked how my kids were doing, but I don't remember ever discussing my family with him for a long time."

"Did you handle Greg's personal matters, like his checking account?"

"No, Greg had his own way of doing things. He not only kept his personal matters to himself, but the firm's too. He had everything on his laptop. I was so concerned that I made him back up his laptop twice a week with a cloud service. I didn't have anything to do with his money. The bitcoin purchase surprises me, for instance."

"That's all for now, Rose. Does anyone have any questions?"

The lawyer for the insurance company spoke up. "Mrs. Mendoza, did you know that Greg was taking out the insurance policy?"

"Not at first, but I knew that Greg had a medical exam that must have been for the policy. He told me that he was going for an annual checkup a week before he got it. I didn't know that there was a policy until Mr. Mariner told me."

"Thanks."

I quickly realized that I'd been moving along without even introducing the insurance policy. That had to be next. I called up the insurance executive to testify. He related that Greg had purchased the insurance policy three months prior to his death. He paid thirty-eight hundred and change for it. His medical examination showed nothing unusual except for slightly elevated blood pressure, not unusual for a financial executive in the midst of turmoil. To everyone's surprise, the check with which he paid for the policy was drawn on a Robertson Investments account. That would complicate bankruptcy matters depending on Judge Wiseman's decision.

After that testimony, I asked Sara to testify. After she was sworn in, I waded in and asked her to describe her relationship with Greg and his state of mind.

"Yes, as I've told others, Greg and I were not getting along well. My opinion is that Greg's being under such terrible financial pressures explains his bad attitude. I'm sure you'll ask me whether his demeanor changed shortly before the aircraft accident, and I'd have to say no to that. To the end Greg acted decisively and with a level head. Not communicative, but not any different than a month or two prior to his death. He didn't tell me specifically that he was in financial difficulty, but I could tell that he was anxious about the markets. No detail. Same with his love affair with the airplane. No discussion of details except how cool it was. For instance, I had no idea he got the maintenance manuals for the plane. I'm surprised he had any interest in that.

"Another thing that bothers me is why he even took a policy out. His brothers and I can get along without the policy proceeds, and given my relationship—or rather the lack of it—I wonder why he even would name me as a beneficiary. Over a year ago he gave me enough money to be financially independent, and my business has been good to me since then."

I had Sara then address her relationship with Paragon Diamonds, and she repeated what she had previously told me, that she was simply a buyer of diamonds for her business. No other business relationships.

"Frankly, Mr. Mariner surprised me when he told me that Greg had a broader relationship with them. I thought he only picked up diamonds for me and had no other dealings with them. I can understand the powers that be at Paragon wanting to know where their investments stood."

"Mr. Stonewater will testify that the telephone records they got from Paragon and Minardi showed that you had long discussions with Minardi right before Greg's death and right after. Would you explain that?"

"I'm sorry that I wasn't exactly forthcoming with you before. Sal called me when Greg started stonewalling him and asked me to intervene with Greg on his behalf. I didn't want to get in the middle of Greg's deals with Paragon, but Sal told me that Greg had bought diamonds and had not fully paid for them. I didn't know what to do. That was right before Greg dying. Basically I told Sal I couldn't and didn't want to do anything. Sal got frustrated after talking to me for a long time. Then after Greg died he harassed me again, trying to get me involved in getting his money back. I told him I was powerless to do that, that I was not involved in Greg's business in any way. He was not a happy man but left me alone after that.

"Then what capped everything was Mr. Mariner telling me that he suspected that Paragon's diamonds were not certified, that they'd been smuggled into the country. Gave me an entirely new perspective on Paragon. Mr. Mariner told me not to deal with them anymore, so I stopped. I had plenty of inventory for my jewelry and only recently had to find new sources. Prices have gone up substantially."

Again I asked if others had any questions. They did not. We moved on—to me.

The court reporter swore me in and I began pontificating. I related the details of my involvement. The whole thing. Smokey Hundley, the diamond treasure, and my three or four meetings with Greg over a period of two years.

"The mystery to me stems from the way Greg acted. During the entire period I knew him, Greg didn't change. At no time did he seem other than calm and together. His enthusiasm was infectious, whether it had to do with his airplane, his Bloomberg terminals, politics in Blanco, or whatever. When he finalized his codicil he was all business and anxious to get back to his financial world."

Judge Wiseman interceded. "John, do you have an opinion on his death? Murder or suicide?"

"Only a tentative one. We need to focus on the facts we don't know. Who killed Sal? Who tampered with the aircraft? Who really owns the anonymous LLCs? Who was behind the death threats Oliver Stonewater found on Greg's voicemails?"

"Do you think we should wait until we get answers to those questions?"

"I'm not sure we will ever get answers. Oliver?"

Stonewater spoke up. "Look, I've been at this now for six months, and I can't answer John's questions. My team, the New York team and the NTSB have worked this case for months and keep running into dead ends. I've been an agent for twenty years, and it's my experience that when we get to this point in an investigation, the trail gets cold and we can only wait on new information popping up later. We've done everything we can."

"Mr. Stonewater's statement sounds like a good place to end the testimony for now. John, do you have other witnesses?"

"Rob Hall and Paul Streeter to testify regarding the financial condition of the firm and of Mr. Robertson at the time of his death."

"Let's do that tomorrow morning, and then if any of you here in attendance want to add anything or make a statement regarding the cause of death, we should have time for that. For now we will adjourn."

# 23.

I looked forward to the next day. Had dinner with Rob Hall, and we spent the evening telling war stories about our respective businesses. The Robertson affair being out of bounds, neither of us tried to bring the subject up. I missed Carla and the kids. When I went into the conference room the next morning, I could tell that everyone looked forward to finishing the hearing and then finding out what Judge Wiseman thought.

Stonewater motioned for me to go out of the room with him when I arrived.

"John, we have Hundley. He'd been released on bail after local police arrested him. Not too hard to find him though. We called his office number, he called back, and when I told him what was going on, he volunteered to come to the hearing. He said he wanted to make clear that he was not involved with the deaths of Robertson or Minardi."

"Do you have him here?"

"Yep. Got him stashed in one of the offices down the hall if you want to use him."

"Sure do."

I went back to the conference room and announced that a new witness was available, Bart Hundley. Judge Wiseman asked me to bring him in. He made quite an entrance. Obviously out of place. Everyone's image of a tough guy. He looked like the bodybuilder he was, but his face and walk showed that the man had a lot of miles on him. The court clerk swore him in.

"Mr. Hundley…"

"Call me Smokey."

"Okay. Smokey, you and I have met before, in Blanco. Is that correct?"

"Yes." I could tell that Hundley had been a witness before, or at least interrogated. Answered the questions. No elaboration.

"Let's make sure we're on the same page factually. You know that Greg Robertson was killed in an airplane crash. You know also that Sal Minardi was executed mafia-style in New York five weeks ago. Correct?"

"Yes."

"Have you ever been around aircraft?"

Hundley laughed and opened up. "You bet. Besides being on airplanes a lot for my job, when I was a member of Seal Team Two, we spent many hours in helicopters. They even made us learn the basics of operating helicopters in case a pilot was killed or injured."

"Do you have a pilot's license or any licenses to carry weapons?"

"No pilot's license. I operate my business out of Atlanta, mainly because it's so easy to get anywhere from there. I've got Texas and Georgia open carry permits as well as concealed weapon permits."

"Are you armed right now?"

"Yes, I have a snub-nosed thirty-two automatic strapped to my ankle. Routine for me unless I'm going through an inspection at an airport. Never can tell when I might need it."

"Let's get to the heart of it. You were in Blanco for quite a while. What were you doing there."

"Pardon me, but that place is boring. Nothing going on. I was retained by Paragon Diamonds last March. They found me through a friend of mine who's in a similar business. They said they wanted to get some diamonds back that hadn't been paid for. That's all. A repo kind of job. I started in Houston and had an intel services friend look around in Houston online, and he told me that if Robertson was trying to hide the diamonds from anyone, he'd be doing it at his ranch in Blanco. No safe hiding places in Houston since the banks there cooperated with authorities for information. My job turned out to be a toughie when Robertson's plane went down, so I waited a while. Then you, Mr. Mariner, were appointed the executor and I knew it was time for me to go to Blanco. I didn't have a plan or idea for getting the diamonds back, but at least my employer wanted to know where the diamonds were.

"So I went to Blanco, not knowing a soul, and I reconnoitered the area, including your house and your office, your schedule and your family. That's my business. I swear to you that the diamonds were the only thing I was after. They wanted them back. I didn't go there to harm anyone, and I wasn't in Houston during that whole time and was not in Blanco until after the plane went down."

"By reconnoiter do you mean breaking into my house and my office?"

"Sorry about that. I didn't hurt anything. Just looking for the diamonds."

"Okay. I guess that's not important now. Were you in New York city any time after Robertson's death?"

"I hate that place. Too many people per square foot. Everything costs two or three times as much as they do in Atlanta. The answer is no."

"What do you know about Paragon Diamonds?"

"As I told you, they got my name from a friend. Didn't know them and couldn't find a D&B credit report on them, so I made them pay me in advance. Good money. They paid me a thousand a day plus expenses for doing not much of anything except looking around. When I finally got around to figuring out where the diamonds were and leaned on you to give them back, events had taken over and I would have been in big trouble repossessing the diamonds from a bankruptcy court. That's when I told Paragon I couldn't do anything else."

"Were you dealing with Sal Minardi?"

"No. The guy introduced himself as Franklin Smith. Phony name, it turned out. After I finished, it wasn't a week before Minardi was killed. I tried to find information on Paragon after that, but Paragon sort of disappeared. Glad I got paid in advance."

"One final question. Did you take Greg's laptop out of my office?"

Hundley squirmed and leaned over toward his briefcase. "Sorry. I sent it back to you, as you know. Not sure this matters anymore, but I couldn't get into it since I didn't have the password to get in."

"All right, Smokey. I'll let your theft rest, at least for now. That's up to the authorities. Thanks for coming in and clarifying your role in this. I wonder how events would have rolled out had I been able to turn over the diamonds to you."

"Probably Minardi would be alive today."

I thanked God that I wasn't part of Smokey's world. I next had Rob sworn in, and he described the firm and its troubled history, confirming that Greg had been sucked into running a Ponzi scheme when he began hiding investment losses from his clients. It's in the nature of such frauds that once started, perpetrators don't know how to stop robbing Peter to pay Paul but continue to have eternal hope that they'll find a way out.

"Rob, you never met Greg Robertson, but you've looked over the financial records of the firm, his personal finances and files, and his emails and voicemails. Can you give us an opinion concerning his state of mind around the time of the accident?"

"Pure speculation on my part, but I've been in this business a long time and have seen people under dire financial pressures before. This one is as bad as it gets. By the time of his death, Robertson had run out of alternatives. He borrowed money and hid it from the firm's records. He took trading risks that no established trader would take. Since I didn't know him, I can only say he was desperate. It makes sense to me that he might have committed suicide in an elaborate way to cover his tracks. On the other hand, he had to know that even after his death, the true state of his finances would come out. Maybe he didn't want to be around.

"I know that you, Judge Wiesman, have asked others their opinion. I only read about murders in the media. I have no experience with that, but I do know that there's plenty of history regarding revenge killings. I can see that Greg's not paying for the diamonds may have set off a chain of events that led Paragon to want to find out where their money was and how it had done. If they found out the true state of affairs at Robertson Investments, and if those anonymous accounts belonged to the principals of Paragon, murdering Greg would be explainable. That would also explain Minardi's death. Given my background living in a non-violent world, I'd go with the suicide alternative."

I interjected. "But Rob, if he committed suicide, why the large amount of money stashed as bitcoins?"

"I can't answer that. Greg was bright, and the bitcoin account may have simply been a part of an elaborate smokescreen to make his death look like an accident or a murder. If it was suicide, I can't explain that. Suicide is such a foreign concept to me. I can't imagine someone doing that. Can't imagine hurting myself."

The assembled group laughed quietly. "All right," Wiseman said. "I think we have had enough testimony, and Paul Streeter's testimony would largely duplicate what Rose and Rob have already said. Isn't that correct, Paul?"

Paul spoke up. "I didn't notice anything different in the way Greg acted several weeks before his death. He obviously felt pressures, but that goes with the business. Greg acted his normal self. Talkative and outgoing. Always up."

Judge Wiseman took over. "I'd like to thank each of you who have participated in this hearing, or rather, arbitration. By abbreviating the otherwise lengthy determination of the cause of death, this matter can come to a close quickly, except of course for those of you connected with the bankruptcies. That will take time.

"As you know, the standard for my final determination is that of the preponderance of the evidence. That is to say, if the evidence is more likely than not to have been one thing or another, that's the standard for the decision. More than fifty per cent. This is not a criminal proceeding, where the standard, as you know, is a determination beyond a reasonable doubt.

"Having now heard from the witnesses, the issue of whether Robertson was killed or committed suicide is not clearly resolved. The evidence does not suggest a decision for me that is beyond a reasonable doubt. You're thinking that the decision could go one way or the other. You're correct, but I won't tell you which way I'm leaning. I strongly suggest that the insurance company representatives meet here with the listed beneficiaries and the representatives of the firm and the estate to see whether a deal can be worked out. Since we don't know with absolute certainty the cause of death, my decision could be the wrong one. Try getting to an agreement. I'll adjourn the meeting here, and we'll get back together here at ten tomorrow."

I liked Wiseman's directness and his recommendation, but I could tell that most everyone else in the room was unsettled. They'd expected the judge to relieve them of any deliberation and make a decision that would resolve the issue. I led the group that wasn't involved in the settlement negotiations out of the conference room, relieved not to be a part of the discussions. Then again, I would have loved to listen in. We went our separate ways, and I took time for myself, knowing that this whole movie was soon to be over. That evening I went across the street to see the Houston Symphony perform. Good to get away from everything.

# 24.

I woke up the next morning refreshed, looking forward to going home after five days. I treated myself to a big breakfast omelet, but I had it delivered to my room to make sure I didn't have to visit with anyone, especially the participants in the hearing. We assembled at ten to get the word.

"I'll call the meeting to order. Has the group involved in the insurance policy come to any settlement?"

The executive from the insurance company stood up. "Yes, your honor. Late last night we agreed to pay fifty per cent of the policy face value. The beneficiaries will split the fifty per cent equally."

"That is excellent. That concludes this matter."

Rose stood up. "Judge Wiseman, aren't you going to tell us how you were going to rule?"

"No, I'm not. Whichever way I would have ruled, one of the parties would be unhappy with the settlement. Let's just say that I'm glad that I have not had to make a final decision, because any decision would have left me with doubt and uncertainty. We stand adjourned."

We filed out of the room to leave the cleanup matters to the bankruptcy lawyers and trustees. That would take a long time. I called Carla as I drove home, for a change at the speed limit, and told her of the goings on that finished up the case.

"I know you're glad that this is over finally. I am too. Having heard everything you did this week, what do you think was behind Greg's death?"

"That's a question on everyone's mind. If I had been Judge Wiseman, I'd have ruled it a suicide, but I would have pointed out that the decision was close, like fifty-one, forty-nine per cent. We'll never know."

# 25.

Life finally returned to normal. The insurance company paid the settlement to the three parties. I turned over Greg's records and the firm's records to the two law firms sorting out who was entitled to what. I was done.

One chilly day in October, as I was looking for a way to warm up my office, I noticed the small box that Rose had sent me containing the receipts and papers that she'd retrieved from Greg's lower left desk "junk" drawer. I'd forgotten about the package when discussions began to have an arbitration of the cause of death. Curious, I opened the package. The pile of receipts, notes, and tax notices looked not worthwhile to dig through until I remembered that the bitcoin account information had never been found by Rose, Rob or the bankruptcy teams. I poured the pile on my desk, but before that I lugged a small space heater out of my cubbyhole where the coffee bar and refrigerator resided and turned it on right next to me.

As I sorted through the pieces of paper, depositing the irrelevant items back in the box, the receipts reminded me of the picture I had of Greg. To my surprise, I found a number of receipts for gifts, gifts obviously acquired for a woman or women. A letter popped up transmitting a credit card, with a ten thousand dollar limit. The credit card number didn't match any we'd found earlier. Then in the middle of the pile I found a piece of plain paper with Greg's handwriting on it. The handwriting first had an odd website address. Below that was noted "PW HJet1980$". Then below that "Q: Where born?" and by that "Texas city." Below that "First public school" and then "Travis Elementary."

I was out of touch with everyone involved with Robertson by then, so I decided to call Oliver Stonewater. The new credit card and what promised to be the bitcoin account might point to whether Greg had committed suicide or was killed. "Hi, John. What's up? I thought you were done with the Robertson matters."

"I was. Rather I am." I explained what I'd discovered and then gave him the card number and bitcoin information.

"That's great," Stonewater said. "I'll get forensics to take a look at the card and the bitcoin account, if that's what we have, to see what went on. Once I get that information, I'll pass it on to you as well as Susan Becker and Linda Wilcox."

"Good. Thanks, Oliver. Let me know what you find."

"Sure will. By the way, our New York office is still chasing Paragon Diamonds. Best we can tell, the money went through several offshore accounts and ended up in a small Swiss bank. We've been looking at that account for some time, and we think the Minaloa Cartel owns it. Keep that confidential since there'll be a big blowup internationally if we hit the bank."

"I'm glad to be sitting here in the middle of nowhere in central Texas." Stonewater laughed and said goodbye.

Ten days later I got nervous about not hearing from Stonewater. I tried to convince myself that the credit card had been superseded by one we already had known and that the website information was some irrelevant venue. Maybe a dating site if Greg was running around on Sara. Then Oliver called late afternoon that day.

"John, that information you turned up has led to interesting data that's made us reopen the investigation. When I passed the information on to the New York office, they decided to look back at what they had in their data room. Not supposed to tell you, but in late January, more than a month before Robertson's death, our office got a warrant to wiretap the Paragon telephones. Lots of calls, including the ones between Sal and Sara. I thought Sara's testimony at the arbitration didn't hold much water but let it rest then. Now I've gone back and listened closely to what they said. Surprised me. The two of them were in league together but for different reasons. Sal had found out that the Robertson firm was desperate and in financial straits. How I don't know, but he told Sara. Sara, on the other hand, had figured out that Greg had several other female relationships. On top of that, she had access to Greg's checking accounts, something Greg set up long ago. When she saw that Greg deposited three quarters of a million from the firm and then wrote a check to some entity, she checked it out and found that he'd bought bitcoins with it. She and Sal got to talking, and they decided to do Greg in. Sal set up everything and paid for it, but Sara agreed to pay half when she got the insurance policy proceeds. After Greg's plane went down, Sara called to tell Sal and discuss how they'd act when the authorities contacted them. And Sara confirmed she'd pay half when Sal totaled up the amount.

"Of course, before Sara got the insurance money, the Paragon owners, whoever they are, did Sal in. Punishment for the Robertson bankruptcy that lost them so much money. And I'm sure they did it to keep him from telling anyone who the owners of Paragon are and how Paragon was operated. The other conversations on the wiretap were ordinary business dealings. The owners must have communicated with Sal in some other way. Could be weekly lunch meetings or something. End of story."

"Not quite. Are there any bitcoins left? Any revelations about how they were used and what the credit card was all about?"

"The bitcoins are still mostly there. About two hundred are left. Almost a million since bitcoins have appreciated recently. Ironic. The credit card is more interesting. He paid the credit card off monthly with bitcoins."

"You can do that?" I asked.

"Yes, some but not all credit card issuers do take bitcoins. We're familiar with them. People who want anonymity set up an anonymous account and use a burner phone, then go to sites they shouldn't, like porn and snuff sites. Greg didn't do that though. His charges were for department stores, online buying sites like Amazon, and hotel and restaurant charges. Strange that he did that when he had access to firm credit cards."

"Those must have been charges that he didn't want either Rose or Sara to see. Sounds as if he had other relationships."

"Back to Sara. She talked openly about the HondaJet with Sal and even told him about the fuel gauges and such. Must have learned that from Greg. Sal doubted her at first, thinking she was just another mad spouse, but as they talked he must have believed that she was mad enough about Greg's losing the money she had with the firm and with his escapades involving other women. As they say, 'Hell hath no fury like a woman scorned.' The scheme got serious when Greg and Sara had their big blowup and their relationship not only cooled but froze. When she testified, she acted like she didn't know much of anything about the firm and its finances, but from what she told Sal, that was not the case. She might not have known about the two sets of books, but she did know that Greg had taken heavy losses trading. She's more sophisticated than she lets on, and I'm sure she knew about the business going on at Paragon and why she got diamonds so cheap. We still don't know who owns those two LLCs that had so much money with the firm. Sara may have owned one of them. She also should have been worried that her own wealth might be exposed if Robertson Investments went under."

"That's a lot to process. I know I need to keep all this confidential, but what are you going to do?"

"Her lawyer, Bob Rivera, would never let us interview her, so the only thing we can do is try to get a grand jury to indict her for the murder based on the transcripts. No one home at Paragon, so nobody we can indict there."

"Makes sense. Glad I am out of the loop now. Good thing Greg and Sara didn't have children. Getting a conviction won't be easy. If she's convicted, I suppose her two million in insurance could be recovered. Maybe she'll make a plea deal so that the two bankruptcies can sort out who gets what."

"And I am glad we're not going to be involved in that. I'll keep you informed, John. Thanks for giving us the information that allowed us to figure this out. Take care."

Now I felt really done with all of this. I sent the package of papers and receipts to Linda Wilcox as a way of finalizing my being part of the Robertson matter. From here on I would follow the tale of Sara and the bankruptcies in the *Houston Chronicle*.